# Miracles on My Watch

Also by Bianca Podesta

*Scleroderma Coping Strategies*

# Miracles on My Watch

## Bianca Podesta

ARCHWAY
PUBLISHING

Archway Publishing books may be ordered through booksellers or by contacting:

Archway Publishing
1663 Liberty Drive
Bloomington, IN 47403
www.archwaypublishing.com
1 (888) 242-5904

Because of the dynamic nature of the Internet, any web addresses or links contained in this book may have changed since publication and may no longer be valid. The views expressed in this work are solely those of the author and do not necessarily reflect the views of the publisher, and the publisher hereby disclaims any responsibility for them.

Any people depicted in stock imagery provided by Thinkstock are models, and such images are being used for illustrative purposes only. Certain stock imagery © Thinkstock.

ISBN: 978-1-4808-2714-1 (sc)
ISBN: 978-1-4808-2715-8 (e)

Library of Congress Control Number: 2016901441

Print information available on the last page.

Archway Publishing rev. date: 02/26/2016

For Nathalie
&
For Bob

To the glory of God

# Contents

# Foreword

In the early 1990s, when I was the director of faith formation for a large Roman Catholic Church, our parish participated in a pulpit exchange during which we were gifted with an enthusiastic United Methodist minister. Bianca Podesta proved to be not only an excellent preacher, but her vitality and friendliness added much to the service and to the coffee hour that followed. She had been working as a pastoral counselor at the time, and returned to our church later that year to lead a workshop on how to survive the holidays when grieving.

I feel honored to have been asked to write about *Miracles on My Watch*, for, truly, miracles are what you'll find in this volume of essays. Upon receiving the manuscript, I made quick work of each story, swallowing them all in one gulp in order to get an overall feel for the material. Satisfied, I began the entire enterprise again, but this time I considered each essay more slowly, pondering its revelations. I was never disappointed.

Throughout this book we encounter a diverse group of characters whose lives and experiences leave us in mindful reverie. Bianca Podesta's skill in painting vivid pictures allows us to see—really *see*—what's happening in the lives of people who've touched her own life. We become drawn into the scenes she relates and are touched by them as well. Her honest yet lighthearted tone balances the serious nature of what she's dealing with in these essays. Nearly every story is spun around the central core of relationships. Pastor Podesta is always willing to accept people just as they are, often putting herself out for their benefit, and she seems to do so at no cost to herself.

Over the years, I've seen Bianca Podesta in action—singing in a madrigal choir, facilitating groups for pastors, and, most recently, leading retreats for pastoral workers. I've read her previous book, *Scleroderma Coping Strategies*, and highly respect her diligence in researching the disease and her bearing witness to the possibility of living a full life despite the challenges brought on by her condition.

What's built into the trajectory of *Miracles on My Watch*, from beginning to end, is the realization of a life consistent with the desire to be of service to the source of life and to humanity. The essays in this book reveal that, while initially timid about her call to ministry, this pastor grew into her true self due to her experiences with all the small and not-so-small miracles she encountered. The stories don't take her merely from middle age to older adulthood but rather to a new awareness of love and creativity in service. There are lessons to be learned from these essays. I know I will return to them again and again, as this is a book to be treasured and reread.

Lois Ann Barton

Lois Ann Barton, a Sister of St. Joseph of Carondelet, is the author of the daily meditation blog: thesophiacenterforspirituality. wordpress.com, which has had a worldwide readership since 2013. She is also the spiritual director and program director of The Sophia Center for Spirituality in Binghamton, New York.

# Preface

Titles that promise miracles are sometimes a little suspect and likely to be misunderstood. Included in this book are some of the incredible, often confounding events that led to my initial call to ministry and my service as parish pastor and pastoral counselor. With their range of small miracles, these essays are testimony to the presence and power of God in my life and in the lives of people I have known.

Most of these stories began in 2001 when I began making notes about particular experiences. While the stories waited to be told publicly, I focused on preserving them privately, as memories. Uncertain about sharing them with anyone other than a few trusted friends, I realized that an honest telling of these stories would expose my own weaknesses.

My writers' groups cured me of my hesitancy. One group is comprised of two ordained ministers and two ministers' wives (all unrelated). We meet about once a month and offer one another helpful critical support. The other group, since disbanded, was a wonderful mix of two religiously unaffiliated professional journalists, a couple of community-minded Jews, a few self-identified Christians, and one brilliantly literate atheist. Seeing the impact of my narrative on members of such a religiously and philosophically diverse group further encouraged me to collect my essays into a book.

Contacting members of my former parishes and their families was essential in the construction of these memories, as we spent time together going over the details of certain events. I've changed people's names throughout this book, except for those that I obtained permission to use. When referring to counseling sessions, I've changed details in order to protect my clients' privacy.

I'd like to thank the people who generously allowed me to share sacred events from their personal lives. Thanks also goes to theologians A. J. van den Blink, who patiently read and commented on my initial drafts, and Thomas H. Troeger, who, after reading a substantial portion of my later drafts, judged them ready for publication.

I'd also like to express my heartfelt gratitude for the ongoing encouragement I received from members of my lectionary group and from friends and family, especially Diane Tolentino, who remained my computer helper throughout. I'm forever grateful for Barbara Alhart Simon and her eagle eye for detail, and for my son, Blake, who whenever I got stuck, offered the best advice: "Just tell what happened, Mom."

# Introduction

To see God moving in the lives of humans and other creatures means more to me than any of my measurable accomplishments. After formal retirement from the Greater New Jersey Conference of the United Methodist Church at age sixty-two, I continued to serve as a part-time counselor and spiritual director in my New York location where, in 1990, I had been appointed full-time. I enjoyed also serving as interim pastor in the New York upstate area for churches of various denominations, including Presbyterian (USA), United Church of Christ, and ELCA (Lutheran) congregations.

The sixteen essays found in this book, which are arranged in chronological order, mark some of the most incredibly beautiful, happiest, and most difficult times of my life's journey. Among the experiences told here are the appearance of a rainbow of unimaginable proportions; a terminally ill man's encounter with Jesus; a shy, normally composed little girl disrupting a Pentecost service; a wild dolphin becoming a compassionate friend; and a developmentally disabled man, revealed as both poet and teacher, who seemingly humbles everyone he encounters.

These short essays may encourage anyone who's ever called out to heaven for help. I hope that busy seminarians, pastors, *women religious*, committed laypersons, as well as people who are feeling distant from God might find refreshment in these brushes with the holy. For anyone who has taken off on his or her own spiritual journey, I can promise a series of true, unpredictable happenings both inside and outside the common boundaries of pastoral ministry. Within the parish setting, I can imagine groups reading the essays aloud together, coupled with open-ended discussion.

While combining the genres of spiritual memoir and personal essay, I tried to keep autobiographical material from slowing down the narrative or interfering with what God might have in mind. The following outline of my religious history should provide sufficient background for the book's references to my childhood and the shadows over my early adulthood.

I became acutely conscious of God's presence at the age of four, when my mother became very sick. My father boarded me in a convent school and had his aunt care for my younger sister while he worked and felt free to live a playboy's life. A year later, on my mother's return to health, she divorced my father and took my sister and me to live in her family's three-story townhouse. My mother, who had grown up going to a Baptist church, rankled at my sister and I having been baptized

Roman Catholics. Nevertheless, at age eight, I celebrated my first Holy Communion. The summer of that same year, my mother married my stepfather, and we moved to a rural town in northwest New Jersey where we became instant Presbyterians. I took the religious uprooting in stride, as I continued to feel closer to God than to the family that claimed me.

At nineteen I left home to study music, literature, and, later, psychology in New York City. For a while I earned a small income singing in Columbia University's Chapel Choir, but felt light-years away from God. I worked toward mending bridges with my father, whom I hadn't seen since the age of eight, and sought a haven from my growing loneliness in marriage.

Married at twenty-four, I was divorced at thirty, when our son was five—the same age I was when my mother removed me from the convent. My physical and psychic energy were waning. In New York I'd done a great deal of drinking with friends and with my father's and husband's families, unaware that even modest quantities of liquor could damage my immune system, which was compromised due to an as-yet undiagnosed illness. It actually took several miracles to help me recognize my call to ministry. The miracle that tipped the scales is where this book begins.

# Icepack

At the age of thirty-three, I boarded a Greyhound bus with a few hundred dollars in my pocket and headed to the town where I'd spent most of my childhood. Badly shaken from a failed marriage and unresolved health issues, I'd recently quit my job and left my eight-year-old son in the care of his father and his father's new wife. Returning to my mother's house seemed a strange stumbling back into my own childhood.

A physician in town suspected my health issues were due to lupus, but he wouldn't order diagnostic tests because I had no health insurance. I then went to a chiropractor who lived within walking distance of my mother's house and who happened to be blind. He found the knotted muscles between my shoulder blades and the sideways bending of my spine. He prescribed a regimen that included spinal adjustments, and made recommended changes to my diet.

In addition to taking care of my physical health, I began

attending the local United Methodist Church where I found friends and, eventually, employment. A new regional counseling center, supported by area churches, took me on as a counselor, and I developed a small practice. Soon able to rent an apartment and buy a car, I felt overwhelmingly thankful. It was in this spirit of gratitude that I volunteered to be a member of the town's rescue squad. One night, while answering a call with my assigned team, I discovered a hazard of rescue work: I made a mistake that only a rookie would make.

I watched Mike, the squad's crew chief, move an injured woman's hand away from a lump on her forehead so that he could clean the wounded area. Gently, he drew a square of moistened cotton over the inflammation.

"Get me an ice pack, B," he said, calling me by my first initial.

The only female crew member on the town's rescue squad, I responded quickly to every order. A stack of plastic-encased compresses was visible on the equipment shelf. To activate, they must be struck against a hard surface—an instruction too obvious to be included in first-aid training. However, being unfamiliar with the compress, I grabbed a pair of scissors from a hook on the wall, cut a corner of the plastic casing and watched in horror as liquid chemicals spilled out onto the floor.

My face burned from the toxic fumes and from shame. Thanks to the spill, which made our rig temporarily uninhabitable, I had just disabled a first-aid vehicle in the middle of a rescue.

"Okay, everybody out," Mike said matter-of-factly. He wheeled the injured woman down the rig's ramp and into a clearing away from the street. Grabbing another ice pack en route, he struck it against the doorway and then held it against the woman's forehead. Meanwhile, the driver mopped up the chemical mess from the floor and bent down with a handful of paper towels to wipe it dry. As he walked toward Mike, the patient, and me, he lifted his hands, palms up, in a gesture of mock helplessness. A little smile curled around the edge of his mouth. And so began my new nickname.

On my scheduled nights with the rescue squad, a few of the men would stand in the doorway of the squad house waiting for me.

"Icepack! Hey, Icepack!" they'd call out in greeting.

I'd smile and yell back, "Hey, guys!" while cringing inside and hoping they would soon drop it.

Despite some minor setbacks, my life was on the upswing. My avocation as a volunteer rescue worker advanced when I signed up to get certified as an Emergency Medical Technician. After weeks of training and hours of written and hands-on testing, the examiner gave me the envelope that contained my certificate and badge. Before going back to my apartment that night, I went to my mother's house for supper. Dishes done, we sat in the living room where I watched her sew my EMT badge onto the sleeve of a new white shirt.

"You're thirty-five years old," she said. "You should be doing this yourself."

She was right, of course. Although I'd always harbored the ambition to be good enough for my mother, I'd been unsuccessful in my striving. She was a stickler for neatness, for instance, and judged me poorly groomed when I failed to comb the back of my hair. The child I used to be still beckoned from the corners and shadows of my mother's house. Perhaps I thought that by going there again, I could rewrite the family script—make it more welcoming.

I put on my white shirt and stood sideways in front of the hall mirror, admiring the badge's Star of Life and snake emblem. My place on the squad had taken me beyond academia and beyond my haunting sense of failure. Having been condemned a hopeless dreamer early in life, I was learning something practical for a change.

The next morning, a Saturday, I put on my whites and headed to the squad house to help with our annual fund-raiser. We were a small group that morning, so we divided into teams of two and three. Mike and I, the first to arrive at the squad house, paired off, and he drove us in the rig to collect donations. Our objective was to take in enough money and pledges to purchase a second rig. Our two ambulances, low and narrow, had insufficient space for proper patient care.

Mike parked at the end of a row of colonial-style houses. Before we could ring the first doorbell on our list, an emergency call came over the two-way radio. A pickup truck had crashed into a tree just outside of town. We heard the dispatcher announce over crackling static that the victim was unconscious.

We were closest to the scene, and we had the best-equipped rig. Mike turned on the sirens. We drove up a steep hill, a few miles from the center of town, and dispatch radioed another crew member to meet us at the scene.

I sat very still in the passenger seat, sending up a silent prayer: "Dear God, help me. I don't know what I'm doing. I've only worked on a rubber mannequin." In my CPR class, I'd saved many armless torsos—tasting rubber as I breathed air into the dummy's mouth and feeling the depression and release of the springs beneath its chest—but I'd never done CPR on a real emergency transport victim. "Dear God, help me," I continued, keeping up my inner chant: "I don't know what I'm doing. I don't know what I'm doing."

Mike parked the rig a short distance from the red pickup truck, whose front end was wrapped around a tree. I jumped out of the rig, went to the driver's side of the truck, and pushed down on the door handle, relieved to find it wasn't jammed. For a moment or two I couldn't move. My hand felt frozen to the handle as I took in the victim with my eyes and heart. He was a sad-looking man in his fifties, tall and quite thin. His face, pressed flat against the steering wheel, was drained of color. His chin jutted oddly to one side. He was motionless, probably not breathing, and possibly dead. Tiny stripes of blood formed wet tendrils on his cheeks. I backed away from the door while Mike and a newly arrived crew member came with the scoop stretcher to help carry him into the patient area of the rig. On the way to the hospital, Mike and I were alone with our clinically dead transport.

"Start CPR," Mike said evenly—something he'd said hundreds of times but never to me directly. I leaned over the victim and positioned my hands, one over the other, on his sternum. Mike began mouth-to-mouth. I did compressions until my arms ached, using my body weight to make strong, focused pushes. The fifteen minutes it took to reach the hospital seemed like an eternity. Mike and I took turns the whole time we performed CPR: one of us did the compressions while the other blew into our transport's mouth. The rise and fall of the sirens' wail formed an eerie background for our counting as we raced toward the hospital's emergency entrance.

Two nurses and an orderly who was wheeling a portable container of pressurized oxygen met us at the door. Without breaking rhythm, the nurses continued CPR as they brought our transport into a treatment room. Mike and I stood watching from an open doorway, since we weren't allowed inside the treatment room. (We weren't allowed to stand in the doorway either, but we held our positions.) Treatment rooms are restricted to all but hospital staff and registered trainees.

A heavy and tired-looking doctor who was holding a clipboard and stethoscope in one hand came through the far door. The dark suit visible under his white coat suggested he may have been on his way home. He must have received the call about this patient right after dispatch contacted us. The nurses in charge also had to be aware of the time lapse, since the data always went out immediately from dispatch to the hospital.

The nurses kept up with the compressions and oxygen until the doctor, after what seemed to be a cursory examination of the patient, spoke up.

"Stop CPR," he said.

I thought my own heart had stopped. I looked around to see helplessness on every face. *We came through the wilderness for this?* I thought. The intuitive scream coursing through my being came out my mouth.

"No! No! No!" I shouted from the doorway. "He doesn't look dead enough to me!"

I was as shocked as everyone else in the treatment room by my outburst, mostly because of how loud it was. I'd always been the shyest, most timid person in any group and unaccustomed to saying what I thought. I never stood up for myself, let alone for anyone else. I was "Icepack," the brand-new EMT, greener than green, who, until that morning, had never seen a dead body except in a casket.

The doctor's eyebrows shot upward as he turned to face me. His mouth tightened with exasperation. One of the nurses gasped and drew back from the patient's body, her hands suspended for a moment between her rhythmic compressions and their cessation.

I was wrong to speak, to confront the doctor. I knew the rule: Obey the physician's directives. We can perform first aid, transport patients, and carry out certain emergency procedures, but we must always act within the limits of our training.

The doctor turned back to his clipboard and began writing something. In a stroke of crazy fearlessness, I walked into the treatment room, past the nurses, and stood in front of him. I was taller than the stout and weary man, but when I reached him my previously loud voice became meek.

"Would you give me permission to put traction on his head?" I asked, referring to the pulling force that sometimes helps with certain skeletal or muscular issues. My pulse was beating in my ears. My hands were damp with sweat. My breaths were quick and shallow. Whatever happened, I had to carry on. The man lying gray and motionless on the examination table needed only one thing. Without waiting for a response, I walked up to the stretcher, positioned myself behind the patient's head, and stood there, so close to the man whose death the doctor was about to confirm. Recalling the odd angle of the patient's jaw against the steering wheel, I remembered something from my EMT training. The day before, toward the end of my examination, my instructor had demonstrated a new technique. She'd placed a weighted cloth torso on the gym's floor and showed me how to put traction on a victim's head when there was suspicion of a compressed windpipe, which could cut off a person's airway.

"Do what you want," the doctor said. "It's too late."

I took the man's head between my hands. My thumbs were under his chin, and my forefingers curved under the base of his neck, just like my chiropractor's hands were positioned when easing my scoliosis pain. I looked up silently to call upon the God I'd forgotten for so long.

I began to imagine the patient's spirit hovering above the room—the way people who've had near-death experiences have described—and I thought about how this man might be looking down at his poor, broken body.

"You're going to be all right," I articulated soundlessly. I then focused on the body before me. Concentrating with every fiber of my being, I balanced myself, pulling the man's head back toward my chest while taking care to keep the traction even on both sides until I heard a dull click.

The next sound was a nurse crying out "He took a breath!" Then, leaning over him, she pressed both her hands against his chest in a wild sort of way. "And his heart is beating!"

I looked around. The doctor's face had paled. The hospital's antiseptic smell suddenly overwhelmed me. I felt faint and grabbed the back of a metal chair to steady myself.

The doctor looked at me accusingly. "You've broken all his ribs and no doubt paralyzed him from the neck down," he said.

"But he's breathing," I choked. "And his heart is beating."

The doctor's accusation jolted me. I had to get out of there, and fast. I ran all the way back to the squad station, which was more than a mile away. Running helped me breathe.

I got into my little white car with the blue light on the roof and drove straight to my mother's house. I wanted to be alone but not completely alone, just safe. As I passed my mother in the kitchen, I made some excuse about needing a break from work. I went upstairs to the spare bedroom and lay down on the quilted bedspread while still wearing my whites and sneakers.

This was the room I'd returned to more than a year ago as a refugee from New York City. I came here back then looking for protection in the house where as a girl growing up I sometimes couldn't wait to escape. After lying down for a few minutes, I walked over to the desk, where I'd thrown my bag, and took out my logbook to complete the same-day documentation of the day's events, but I was neither ready nor able to write. Putting the logbook back in my bag, I lay down on the bed again. A shiver from everything I'd seen that night coursed through me like a current until sleep unexpectedly took over. I woke to the sound of my mother calling me from the bottom of the stairs.

"Come down right away!" she was yelling, now. "Mike's on the phone. He's been looking all over for you."

I took my time going down the stairs and making my way into the den to pick up the only telephone in the house.

"Icepack," Mike said. His voice was almost tender as he spoke the name I'd resented. "Don't you want to stop by the hospital and meet the man you saved? He has a few broken ribs, but otherwise he's okay."

"He's okay?" I asked. I needed to hear him say it again.

"He has some pain in his chest, in his ribs, you know, but he's talking. He's moving normally. Now, Icepack, why don't you come down to the hospital? Some guys are here from other squads. They want to meet you."

"I can't," I said. "Tell them I didn't save him. Just tell them that." I hung up the phone. I had no idea how that man had been revived after not responding to almost thirty minutes of CPR.

I went back upstairs to the bedroom and lay down on the bed again, trying to process the doctor's disturbing behavior. Could he have been so exhausted he was beyond thinking that this poor man might have a chance? And what did he do after he realized the man was going to make it? Did he fall asleep in his clothes in an upstairs bedroom of his house, unable to bear thinking about it anymore? Did he wake up with a changed awareness of any kind? Or did he stay in his professional disguise, a disguise that covered his true self so completely, he kept it hidden where no one, not even he, could find it?

I then thought about the Hippocratic Oath, which charges doctors to avoid causing harm to a patient. Mike, the nurses, and I—one or all of us—*had* harmed the patient. We managed to break three of his ribs. And I broke a most important rule by interfering with the doctor's orders. What my partners saw as courage was something I couldn't own. The first breath that dying man took after being revived, the first new beat of his stopped heart, was due to much more than my applying traction on his head. His rescue had begun with my confession of ignorance and a desperate prayer. Two dedicated teams remained with him throughout that hour, during which the Spirit conspired to restore his life.

Some months later, as a new counselor in the area, I was

invited to speak about healing on "Women's Sunday" at the local United Methodist Church. I asked my young son and several friends to come in from the city to attend the talk, since I was sure it would be a once-in-a-lifetime event. While reading aloud from my scholarly sermon, I occasionally looked up and into the faces of the parishioners. Their breathing, their listening eyes stole me away from my pages, and I began to speak freely, from memory.

Afterward, the pastor in charge asked me if I'd ever thought of going to seminary.

"No," I said. "Never."

Yet, for more than a year, his question followed me everywhere. It surfaced while I was walking or driving; it looked over the shoulder of my dreams. Eventually I had to admit that I wanted, more than anything, to know more about this saving God.

# When Heaven Came Down

"You'd be going out the door backwards!" An odd analogy, but he did have a point.

The director of the counseling center was referring to my call to parish ministry. I'd walked through the door as a member of the pastoral counseling staff with a PhD in psychology and supervised counseling experience. The director and most of the center's counselors had served as church pastors for years. They regarded their clinical training as having freed them from the often harsh demands of parish life and allowed for their economic advancement.

The psychiatrist who led one of our supervision groups recommended that I slow down in making a decision. "Take a couple of courses first," he said. I promised I would and immediately applied to the summer school program at Princeton Theological Seminary.

Princeton's campus is an architectural wonder. Old stone buildings stand like castles on a vast expanse of green. The morning of my arrival, I wandered for more than an hour along curved paths, enjoying every flower, every birdcall until a wave of fatigue sent me back to the moss-covered castle that housed my dorm room. An early wakening and the long drive south had done me in. I lay down on one of the twin beds and slept.

I was awakened by the sound of a key turning in the lock and someone entering the room. After I came to, I realized it was Ellen, the first clergywoman I'd ever met. She'd been involved in developing the pastoral counseling center back home. Upon discovering that we'd both signed up for summer courses at Princeton's seminary, we agreed to share a room.

"You don't have to get up," Ellen said, gesturing for me to stay put as she placed her suitcase by the other bed. It was two o'clock in the afternoon.

I shut my eyes and lay there a little longer, trying to preserve the deep-boned relaxation of restorative sleep before stretching to rouse myself.

"Driving wiped me out," I said.

Ellen didn't respond, which struck me as odd. She'd always been so friendly. I watched her move about, opening closet doors and folding her clothes before putting them away. Her few effortful sighs alerted me, but I waited for her to speak. Leaning over the edge of my bed, I unzipped my duffel bag and shook out the shirts and slacks I'd rolled into tight bundles. I put them on hangers, hoping the humidity would melt the wrinkles by morning.

Ellen finally began to speak in a hushed voice. As we

unpacked our clothes, she unpacked her grief. She told me her two-year-old niece had been killed in a car accident the previous week. Keeping busy while we talked was apparently less awkward for her than sitting face-to-face. We'd never been alone together, and her pain was fresh. I listened as we continued to walk past each other, hanging up our clothes and opening or closing drawers.

After having supper in the cafeteria, Ellen showed me a photograph of her niece standing on grass with the sun in her hair. As she tried to speak the child's name, her voice failed. Throughout the rest of our stay Ellen seldom talked about the child, but her occasional long sighs would remind me of her grief. At night, while lying in bed, I'd think of the tiny girl with the sun in her hair. Trying not to see it, but seeing it all too well, I'd imagine the sanitation truck rolling backward, its driver unaware of the small child running into the street behind it.

When we weren't eating meals or attending morning chapel, Ellen and I were studying. Between classes, I'd walk around campus, a willing captive of the beautiful summer days. Sometimes I'd sit or lie on the grass underneath a tree and read or go over my notes, thoroughly content.

One afternoon I was sitting at my desk, slightly hypnotized by the sound of a steady rain. When the rain stopped, I got up and opened the windows to let in the cooler air. A few minutes later, high-pitched, chirp-like sounds rose from outside the cluster our buildings known as the quad. I quickly realized that the sounds were *human* sounds—exclamations clipped by surprise.

A moment later I heard a number of casement windows being opened, their old cords scraping from the strain, so I got up to see what was going on. Standing at my window, I kept very still for fear that too quick a motion would disturb the amazing sight.

"Look!" I exclaimed, although no one else was in the room with me, and heard in my own voice the beginning of a chirp.

The rainbow enclosing the quad was thicker and brighter than any I'd ever seen. It seemed close enough for me to run out and touch it. Resting flush with the ground at one end, its curve bent upward—extending just above the height of the chapel—and came down to earth on the other side. The curve of the rainbow's color bands looked pavement-solid and spanned the entire quad like a great shielding arm, its wide bands of color cleanly separated, not bleeding or fading into the neighboring sky as do rainbows seen from a distance. Opacity gave the rainbow the appearance of having weight, as though a huge crane might have lowered it carefully onto this exact spot. The grass in front of the quad, landscaped into neatly angled patches, shone like emeralds beneath the rainbow's base.

More than light and air constructed this rainbow. Even if there was no Noah story in the Bible, no promise of a covenant symbolized by a rainbow, promise is precisely what beamed from this arc's breadth and brilliance. This monumental reality spanning the space between four buildings revealed beauty beyond imagining. I opened my window wider and reached out my hand in a futile effort to get closer to the bow's edge, which glowed like the rim of heaven.

The rainbow lasted for only a few more breaths, less than a minute altogether. The chirps and squeaks of the others who'd witnessed it ceased as the huge bright bow began to fade. Having offered us this sudden, substantial view of paradise, the rainbow was now just a gossamer outline. And then it was gone.

That evening, while Ellen and I sat at one of the long, impersonal cafeteria tables, two undergraduates coming back from the salad bar with coleslaw and piles of chips sat down and looked at us sideways, the way young men look at their mothers when we invade their space.

"Did you see the rainbow?" I asked them.

"Yeah, it was something else, right?" one of them answered and then turned back to his chips.

Ellen and I couldn't compare notes about the "Technicolor Promise" that landed on our doorstep because she'd been holed up in the library all afternoon. For me, the rainbow brought immediate relief from the stress of so many assignments. I wanted to celebrate, but since I had a paper due the next morning I was grateful to be able, rather quickly, to weave my thoughts around those of the week's process theologian.

When we got back to the dorm following supper, Ellen got into her pajamas and began reading in bed. I was anticipating one of her long, drawn-out sighs while I finished my paper, but for the first time since we began rooming together, that sigh never came. She eventually broke the silence to say she'd felt better that day than on any day since her niece's death. The tight line around her mouth had disappeared—and she hadn't even *seen* the rainbow.

We sat facing one another on our beds, cross-legged, like friends who'd known each other forever. Our conversation went on for about an hour, soul to soul. She talked about the sadness her niece's death had brought to her family. I told her about my thankfulness for being delivered from past mistakes. In this mutual flash of middle-aged innocence, her grief was eased, and I felt the assurance of forgiveness for thoughtless acts in my former life.

After turning out the lights, Ellen and I fell asleep like two children under the now invisible arc of a rainbow that had seemed as brilliant and solid as a glass prism, yet soft enough to walk on.

# The Yellow Truck

On the day of the accident, I was making the three-hour drive from Drew Theological School to my student church, where I served as a licensed local pastor on weekends and holidays. From Tuesday until Friday, I took classes at Drew Theological School. On the drive that day I listened to recordings of flutist James Galway playing works by Telemann. I was feeling happier than I could remember. Falling in love with God had changed my life trajectory. The only downside was the 200 miles it put between me and my son in New York City. His father's wife had become a second mother to him, but he was a young teen, and my heart knew he still needed me.

As the outside temperature warmed, I cracked open a window to smell the freshness of the autumn air. Another hour and a half of driving before I would arrive at my parsonage near the Delaware River. I looked forward to being there, to seeing the pine-paneled study and the straggly purple flowers by the front door. The town where my parsonage was located—with its two churches, one gas station, and small post office—was one where, according to the locals, not much happened. Franciscan Fathers served the wood-frame church next door. The village's main road ran alongside the river and wound down to a cluster of modest houses in the valley.

After years of taking subways and buses in New York City, I was a cautious driver, obeying every road sign. I'd already passed the area of heaviest traffic along my route and was approaching a junction that led to a relatively quiet stretch of highway. Stopping for a red light at an intersection, I looked up the steep hill to my left where there was another set of traffic lights. I then focused my attention on the yellow pickup truck in front of me. When our light turned green, I followed the truck as it advanced a few feet—until it suddenly stopped short. I saw the driver staring wide-eyed into his rearview mirror, and I slammed on my brakes. An 18-wheeler Mack truck coming from the left was unable to stop at the red light. Speeding down the hill, it struck the yellow truck with such force that both vehicles flipped over. Each now lay on its side on opposite shoulders of the highway.

About twenty yards separated me from the yellow truck, and an additional twenty yards between me and the Mack. Everything was eerily silent. I feared what might happen next. As my awareness sharpened, I noticed the oncoming traffic at the top of the hill slowing down, and cars stopped, forming a growing line. A few drivers who were anxious to leave the scene wove slowly around the disabled trucks, while the drivers lined up behind me had turned off their engines.

Reviewing my own condition, I knew I was alive and that my fingers were wrapped tightly around my car's steering wheel. The veins on my forearms stood out like welts. After taking a few deep breaths, I released my grip on the wheel. *What happened to the two truck drivers?* I wondered as I watched both vehicles for signs of life.

The upside door of the yellow truck eventually opened and slowly inched skyward. First a hand and then an arm emerged as the driver pulled himself out. He jumped down onto the road and walked toward me. Behind him, farther away, the driver of the Mack truck made the same unbelievable escape, exiting the upside door apparently unharmed. As the driver of the yellow truck approached my car, I got out to meet him. He told me that when he saw the eighteen-wheeler coming down the hill, he knew that if I kept following him, I'd be "killed in that little car." He reassured me he would "take it from there" and that there was no reason for me to stay, since I wasn't directly involved in the accident.

Waving his hand in the direction I was heading, he dismissed me kindly with words I couldn't remember when I tried to recall them in the immediate aftermath. It took me quite a while to respond, as I was still stunned from what I'd experienced. He waited patiently next to my car as I struggled to find the words to thank him. I leaned against the hood to write his name and address on a scrap of paper. I knew I would need, somehow, to thank him again. If he'd stepped on the gas instead of the brake, he would have beaten the Mack truck through the intersection, but I would have been killed.

Feeling short of breath, I left the site, crossing the intersection and making a left onto a road that wound through fields and farmland. For the last part of my journey, I had no sense of time. I listened to no Galway; I didn't chatter on to God. The serene tree tapestry that lined the road had been shredded by the fear vibrating along my nerve endings. I'd come closer to my own death than I ever had been. It would take more than a thank-you note to acknowledge the intervening power.

When I arrived at my parsonage, its facade looked flat, like a child's drawing. The purple flowers played their staccato by the door, unheard. Walking from room to room, I sensed a hollowness, a haunting. The comfortable old furniture I myself had painted and upholstered offered little comfort. This place no longer seemed like my own dear home. What could I do to bring things back to normal? Attempting to orient myself, I asked questions of the air: Should I find something to eat? Call a friend? I was walking and thinking in circles.

At last, I phoned Frank and Dot, a retired minister and his wife—good friends. They lived less than a mile down the road. Nearly every Friday evening I'd go there for supper, so it was natural for me to invite myself to their home. Their food and their friendship restored me and helped to soothe the aftershock of my experience.

When I got home, I had a sermon to prepare. The reading for Sunday morning, from the Gospel of Luke, happened to be about the Samaritan who, at his own peril, stops to assist a man who had been beaten, and was lying in the road, left for dead.[1] Religious rules and fear keep a priest and a Levite, who first encounter the man, from trying to help him. A traveler from Samaria is the only one who comes to his aid. He binds up the man's wounds, puts him on his own donkey, cares for him at an inn, and pays for his follow-up care. Jesus' question—while relaying this story—asks which of the three men was neighbor to the victim, and is intended to make us reflect on our own reasons for not helping people in need.

Luke's story took me back to those moments after the crash. In the context of danger on the road, my "neighbor" was the driver of the yellow truck, who put himself in the way of death for me. He anticipated that if I were to follow him across the highway, my car would be in the path of the Mack. I understood then, and understand now, that his decisive impulse was an example of how God works through human beings.

That Sunday, my student church was nearly full, with about 45 people in attendance. The sun shone through the stained-glass windows in shafts of colored light onto the faces of the congregation. I stood before them in my flax robe and deacon's stole. My notes remained on the lectern untouched for the hour. After reading the Gospel aloud and then giving reasons

---

[1] Lk 10:25–37

for the inaction of the priest and the Levite, I gave reasons for the times we, too, fail to act on others' behalf.

I then told the congregation about my narrow escape on the road and the driver of the yellow truck. I was the stranger for whom he risked himself. With this realization charging through my soul, I felt the wetness of tears on my face. They were tears of recognition, not sadness. My purpose in life— postponed for so long and so mixed with other strivings— was finally, unmistakably confirmed. I was in the world to do some good. This knowledge came with a suspension of time and place. In that moment, I was no longer standing in front of my congregation; I was standing at the edge of a highway intersection face-to-face with the driver of the yellow truck. He was saying the words, forgotten until now: "You are free to continue on."

# A Baptism

As a new pastor, I was shaken by the tenderness I felt for each baptismal candidate. It didn't matter whether it was a screaming infant, or a lanky twelve-year-old from my confirmation class, or a tattooed reformed sinner who'd lived on the street—every one of them was fragile. They were all babies with innocent eyes, and they all wanted to be friends with Jesus and held in the arms of God.

When I'd draw the watery cross on each forehead, the swelling I'd feel in my throat suggested that I, the baptizer, was as fragile as any supplicant and that the Holy Spirit had spilled some of its light on me as well. Becoming conscious of my own infancy, I couldn't fathom how I'd been called from a life of missteps to such a great honor.

Although I felt tremendous joy at the ceremony, I knew that baptism was serious business. Prior to each one, I made a home visit. Jonathan Henry's parents had transferred to my parish from another United Methodist Church because it was closer to their new home. The three of us went over the entire ritual, including its meaning and what it was they were promising to do. Saint Paul's teaching about living and dying with Christ is difficult to convey when there's only a sprinkling or pouring of the baptismal water. Some denominations wait until a child is twelve years of age for a whole-body immersion. For me, being held under the surface and then lifted out of the watery depths evokes the River Jordan—or at least a baptismal water tank. Jonathan's parents and I talked about their bringing up Jonathan in the faith, their involvement in the church community, and their promise to model kindness and justice for their child.

During my visit, I picked up Jonathan and held him on my knee. Like most eight-month-old babies, he was at least double his birth weight. Although he was born in November, his parents postponed his baptism until the summer to accommodate out-of-state relatives who'd have to travel to attend the ceremony.

On Jonathan's big day, I asked the children in the congregation to gather around the baptismal font. One boy stood on tiptoe while holding onto the rim of the dark oak stand with both hands. He looked into the silver bowl as though it contained some mysterious treasure. Another boy touched the side of the pitcher I was pouring from, while a small girl opened her tiny star hand and placed it in the water's path.

I had begun to develop a children's message for these occasions. "I can baptize with water," I'd say, "but only God can baptize with the Holy Spirit." *Baptize* was a word or concept that six-year-olds could understand, since there was water and a font to illustrate its meaning, but *Holy Spirit* called for an example every time.

"The Holy Spirit is invisible, like love," I'd say. "You can't see it, but sometimes you can feel it, like the way you can feel the wind when it blows against your cheek."

I'd reach toward a child I knew well and brush his or her cheek lightly with my hand. A murmur would run through the group, as the children were now both alert and perplexed. I'd pause, smiling into their upturned faces, and they'd watch me with eyes clear as glass. I had to be careful, because if I said too much, I'd lose them.

"Jesus is here, and will be here with us the whole time," I'd tell them reassuringly.

They'd recognize Jesus' name. "Oh, yes!" their faces would answer.

The children would grin when I'd tell them how, from the moment of their baptism, people in the congregation become their extra mothers and fathers and their extra grandmothers and grandfathers. When preparing for Jonathan's baptism, I told them that, after I poured the water on his head, Jonathan would be their brother. An older child who had two brothers at home reached for the microphone I was using to correct me. "*Extra* brother!" he declared loudly.

For the most part, the children anticipated Jonathan's baptism in silence. They stared with fascination at Jonathan, whose sailor suit and white leather shoes made him look more like a large boy doll than a baby. No Christening gown for this little man, who was ruddy and seemingly ready to be tested by life at sea.

I took Jonathan from his father's arms. When I lifted him during my home visit, I'd felt a sharp pull in my lower back. This time I wedged him into the crook of my arm. To hold him securely, I had to balance his backside on my hip to position his head over the font.

After reading the liturgy, I followed the practice of asking his parents his name.

"Jonathan Henry," his father answered.

I scooped up water with my hand and poured it over Jonathan's forehead, saying the words I knew by heart while imprinting the invisible cross.

Jonathan's black curls glistened with drops of the sacramental water, and, given his normally happy temperament, I expected him to be well-behaved throughout the ceremony. I think now of my favorite hymn for a baptism, John Ylvisaker's "I Was There to Hear Your Borning Cry,"[2] when we have the chance to get teary-eyed while singing God's promise to be with this child, as God has been with us, and will be with us through every stage of our living and dying.

I was therefore surprised as this new creature in Christ started to screw up his face in what appeared to be preparation for a mighty scream. Rocking him a little, I thought that maybe

---

[2] Ylvisaker, John. "I Was There to Hear Your Borning Cry." © 1985. Used by permission. John Ylvisaker, Box 321, Waverly, IA 50677

he'd remember me from when I was holding him a few days earlier. Instead, he shut his eyes tightly and turned his head away from the towel I was using to wipe the water from his face. His little chest rose under the white sailor collar. Fearing he was about to wail, I sank into what I hoped was loving submission as I watched him complete a long inhalation.

While bracing myself for that first piercing yell, I saw Jonathan's lips curl into a smile, and then a tinkling laugh emerged. It came lightly at first, almost feathery, and increased to a rippling crescendo. As he grew conscious of its effect, Jonathan's vocalization took on variations. First it was high and sweet, like a tune struck on crystal. Then, as he found his deeper voice, chest tones broke through. Because of the church's acoustics, the sound traveled by echo, reaching up into the building's wooden beams. At the sound's climax, a thrilling staccato filled the little sanctuary like wild flute music.

After glancing up at me to see if it was all right, the church-school children shyly joined in with their own laughter. As instant conductor, I encouraged the older children to join in. A handful of teenagers coughed and snickered, covering their mouths from embarrassment until they simply let go. Male voices, straining toward maturity, offered a bit of baritone. Sticking out among the higher sounds, they added depth to the chorus.

Caught up in the moment, the whole congregation began to laugh. Even the old folks, whom one child referred to as "the ones with snow on their heads," succumbed. All this laughter, moving upward, pressed against the light-flooded windows. It cascaded down walls and ricocheted off the corners of the pews. For several glorious minutes, the little wood-frame church seemed to be shaking with the joy of it. It was as if suddenly we had been freed from years of holding back something from the universe within us, something we never recognized as part of our walk with God.

# Music for an Easter Morning

"**D**id you forget I'm blind, you dimwit?"

I was laughing because I knew I deserved that. My mother had every right to guard herself against my crazy idea. That telephone conversation, which took place late one Good Friday afternoon, began with me asking her to fill in as the organist at my church on Easter morning. Admittedly, my request was a practical improbability. She lived three hours away, was completely blind in one eye, and would likely lose sight in the other from diabetic retinopathy.

Helga, my church's regular organist, said she needed more time to get used to the new instrument that was installed only the day before. Our music committee hired a guitarist, but the thought of all those alleluias being accompanied by a single guitar dismayed me. I wanted my first Easter as sole pastor to rock, with the organ's flute and horn stops pulled out for the fullest sound. Helga had expressed reasonable concerns about playing the new organ so soon, but my mother had been a musical athlete since early childhood. She had to retire from playing viola in the New Jersey Symphony, but still taught violin and piano at home, and played these instruments by ear as well as from a score until she lost her vision.

Undeterred, I kept talking and trying to win her over. I told her that the way the lid of the organ's cabinet's slid down into the back of the frame was just like the old roll top desk she had in her den; I told her how Helga was so overwhelmed by the organ's size and complexity, she wasn't able even to touch the keys and how she switched the "on" button and, seeing the instrument's front panel light up, cried, "It looks like the cockpit of a 747!"

My imitation of Helga's accent, which was meant to amuse, was met with silence.

I persisted anyway. "You may be blind," I said, "but you don't need to *see* to play the piano. You'll be playing only the first hymn; the guitarist can play the others. Come on, Mother. What do you think?"

"I'm not an organist," she said firmly.

I felt like a bully, but was too invested to back down. "It's the same keyboard as the piano," I argued, telling her what she already knew but still hoping she'd change her mind. Music was our primary bond. I remember my delight when, at my urging, she agreed to exchange my dance classes for voice lessons. Performing was the one thing we could do together without conflict. She would play piano or violin while I sang. Any other form of interaction seemed to die in its tracks. When

I was a child, she'd often look at me, frown, and then look away. "You're the image of your father," she'd say" and follow it immediately with, "He was a son of a bitch!"

I had no way to compare my father's face to mine and no memory of his alleged meanness. Empty paper frames in our old family albums suggested my mother had cut him out of photos just as deliberately as she had cut him out of our lives. My younger sister and I were six and eight when our mother remarried. Determined to make us an intact family, she changed our surnames to our stepfather's when she registered us for public school and selected a church for us to join. I settled into the new family constellation with certain misgivings.

My father would occasionally drive to where we lived and park under the trees outside the school. Unlike my sister, I saw him there, and every time we walked home I'd look far over my left shoulder and squint, in hopes of catching a glimpse of him through the car's darkened windows.

Convincing my mother to substitute as Easter Sunday organist grew entirely from my misplaced pastor's pride. The phone call wasn't going as I'd hoped. I listened as my mother complained about my not understanding the hardness of her life since my stepfather died. This monologue, intended to discourage me, brought my frustration to the breaking point. After she finished, I said what I never could have said to poor Helga: "But you *have* to play; you just *have* to!"

My mother sighed. "You want to take me all the way up to New York State and back, a couple of hundred miles, to play the organ for your service. What are you thinking? I'm not well. I can hardly take care of myself."

If she was talking, that meant she was softening.

"I can be there tomorrow at noon," I said. "I'll help you pack. I'll cook our meals, and make your snacks. You'll see— we'll have a nice visit."

"I'm not an organist," she said again, but in a quieter voice, acquiescing.

My mother had legitimate reasons to refuse my request. Although her vision was partially restored by laser treatments, her orchestra days were long over. She had to read from enlarged copies of musical scores in order to continue playing in a local quartet. Her eyesight wasn't the only problem though. With any change to her schedule, her diabetes could get out of control, which would mean trips to the emergency room. And I was worried about her emotional ups and downs, too. Grief over my father's long-ago estrangement seemed to have seeped into her bones. As is not uncommon, the death of my stepfather, her fair and reliable second husband, created space for the mourning of an earlier devastating loss.

Finally, Mother reluctantly agreed to help me out. After we said our good-byes and hung up, I began preparing for the next two days before going early to bed.

Holy Saturday dawned cool and clear. The traffic on the way to New Jersey was light, and I arrived at my mother's house before noon. The two of us sat at the old kitchen table eating tuna fish sandwiches and canned cream of mushroom soup, my once-favorite lunch. My mother complained intermittently about the impracticality of our trip, and I tried to sympathize without causing her to change her mind. Later, she raved quietly as I folded and packed her best polyester pants suit and placed her insulin, needles, and syringes in a big wicker basket. While stuffing the empty spaces in the basket with ice-filled plastic bags, I addressed her concerns as reasonably as I could.

"Look," I said, "the first hymn is the only hymn you have to play. Everybody knows it; everybody loves it. I'll sing descant with the choir on the last verse." At that, I noticed a faint upturn at the corner of her mouth. Encouraged, I carried on.

"For the prelude and postlude, you can play any piece you know or any hymn with a little ornamentation."

Confident about my mother's ability to perform, I worried only about her ability to take pleasure in the experience. She still played piano at family gatherings, but I'd noticed her other avenues of pleasure closing off. She saw less of old friends. The year after my stepfather died, she began to regard their seven-year-old son as "the man of the house." Years later, my sister moved out, and our half-brother continued to fill Mother's house with a male voice and presence. The affection they shared postponed her loneliness until he, too, left to begin a life of his own.

While Mother and I were on the highway heading northwest, she repeated her line about not being an organist. She meant, specifically, that she wasn't a pipe organist or a church organist, since she'd played pump and electronic organs and always kept her old accordion, a souvenir, on the floor of our hall coat closet. I continued to reassure her that she was a natural on the keyboard and that once she got used to my church's organ she'd be fine. Neither of us seemed capable of ending this queer duet; it went on and on until our bathroom stop, when I came to my senses and put a CD of string quartets into the CD player.

Upon our arrival, I got out of my car and walked around to the passenger side to escort her into my parsonage. Early that morning I'd picked a bunch of forsythia for the guest bedroom where she'd be sleeping. The light from the window shone bright enough for her to see the buttery yellow flowers fanning outward. At four o'clock we snacked on ripe pears and brie and then walked slowly across the lawn to the church. My mother placed her hand on my arm for support.

After approaching the organ, my mother ran her palms over its cabinet as if she were trying to predict the quality of sound the instrument would make. She sat on the bench without a word of complaint. Unlike Helga, my mother didn't react when I pressed the power button and the panel lit up with slot-machine brightness. Although sensitive to light, my mother was unfazed by the display of the organ's glowing buttons and multiple stops. There, in the sanctuary, she seemed almost content as the darkness of the late afternoon fell around us like a cloak.

I identified the stops and pulled the ones she chose—horns and flutes, which are also my favorites. After she found the little shelf for resting her feet, she played for about an hour. I stood by, watching her confidence build, her back straighten, and her sad blind-lady victim face relax and become pleasantly focused. The hymn at the center of this complicated undertaking is in the key of C and easily adaptable to spontaneous harmonies. I sang impromptu counterpoint in the hope of making my mother smile.

After supper, my mother and I hugged goodnight. She watched television in her pajamas with one of the many afghans she'd crocheted for me pulled up to her chin while I went over my sermon in the little study just off the living room. Tired from the 250-mile round-trip, my observance of the Holy Saturday vigil consisted of drifting prayers that ushered me into a deep sleep, which lasted until six o'clock the next morning.

My mother stayed inside the parsonage to have breakfast and manage her insulin while I headed to the church yard to conduct a sunrise service that included a reading from the Gospel of John about Mary Magdalene's encountering the resurrected Jesus.[3] While I stood there shivering in my long white dress, I was overcome by my sense of the reading being more than just a reading, and my prepared proclamation, more than just a telling. I felt, in those moments, to represent the spirit of the real Mary Magdalene in the old churchyard, surprised by the risen Lord.

The eleven o'clock congregation rustled with anticipation, quieting down only when my mother began to play some Bach

---

[3] Jn 29:11–18

she remembered from childhood. The crisp piece, with its finely separated notes, required no pedal work. A stirring of love tempted me to think that the events of this weekend might be the beginning of us seeing each other differently. I'm not sure why, but my mother's way of introducing me to people as "my daughter, the Methodist minister" made me cringe. I imagined that if I were to accept my mother's being proud of me, I would have to deny her indelible disappointment in me, as well. Surely, if things were to change between us, she would want me to understand what she went through—the thankless mothering of three children, two of whom were born out of a marriage that broke her heart.

The opening hymn with its horn and flute accompaniments brought forth joyous alleluias from the congregation. After the scripture readings and prayers, the guitarist we'd hired cleverly engaged the children in song. His strumming of the later hymns went smoothly, if slightly awkward within the Easter Sunday context.

My message that day had a smaller, untold resurrection story running parallel to the big one. It was the story of how a nearly blind woman, confined by her disability and her sorrow, had come back to life in the service of God and her elder daughter's faith community. I dared to believe we were closer than we'd ever been.

I prepared lunch soon after the service had ended intent on keeping my promise to get Mother home before suppertime. The drive to New Jersey, during which she mostly slept, brought a welcome silence that helped me unwind from the morning's effort.

After arriving at my mother's house, we ate sandwiches and salad in the kitchen. Later, as we stood at the back door and said our good-byes, I saw a great weariness in her face. I thanked her for what she'd done and hugged her close.

"Don't ever ask me to do that again," she said. I stepped back.

"Okay, I won't," I answered, and never did. I didn't have to. From then on, my churches hired organists from the Guild and kept a list of substitutes for emergencies.

My last musical performance with my mother rang out a dozen winters later from the recreation area of the nursing facility where she was living. My husband, Bob, pushed my mother's wheelchair close enough to the communal piano so that she could reach its keys. Our only listeners were the patients shuffling down the hall and pausing for awhile near the doorway. The following year, two days after Christmas, my mother died in a local hospital. Her violin and viola, which she'd used to accompany hymns in the nursing home's chapel, were secure in their green velvet-lined cases under her bed, ready for my sister and me to inherit.

By then I'd come to understand and accept my mother's and my differences. My desires were not her desires, and our decades of playing and performing together could never bridge the gulf that existed between us. After all, that particular Easter Sunday, she'd said, "Don't ever ask me to do that again." At the time, those words seemed like a death knell, but now that I'm older, I wonder if she was simply worn out from the strain of traveling and performing.

It always seemed that nothing I could do would alter my mother's perception of me. I would always be the selfish daughter who lived at a distance and resembled my abandoning father in more ways than one. Years of psychotherapy, first as patient, then as counselor, failed to fill the void my mother's dissatisfaction had created in me. Even when I was at seminary, immersed in the science of forgiveness, I remained a shaky beginner in the realm of relationships.

On my mother's last Christmas Day, I woke up early to drive to the hospital, a single magus with three gifts—to find an early Epiphany. No frankincense, no myrrh, but I'd promised to bring gold in the form of homemade shrimp cocktail—and that's where I failed her. Shrimp cocktail seemed like such a crazy gift, considering her condition, so instead I brought homemade turkey broth. I didn't realize my mistake until I took the lid off the thermos and its aroma reached her nose.

"Where's my shrimp cocktail?" Mother asked sharply.

"I thought this would be easier to digest," I said, sounding like a bad parent even to myself. The effects of end-stage kidney failure left my mother barely able to swallow the sips of broth I fed her with a spoon. But a shrimp cocktail—just the salty-sweet smell of it, the tart taste of horseradish on the tip of her tongue—would have been enough, more than enough, for a token feast.

Despite her disappointment about the broth, Mother received my second gift, a holiday sweatshirt covered with green trees and red ribbons, quite happily. I borrowed scissors from a nurse and cut the back of the sweater open from top to bottom so that it would fit over the tubes and wires attached to her body. We both knew this would be a one-time wearing. Now dressed in holiday gear and perfunctorily fed, my mother opened my third gift: an eleven-by-fourteen photograph of my infant granddaughter, Olivia, her first great-grandchild.

She held the photo in her hands for quite a while, turning it in all directions, catching the sunlight from the window with her working eye. What she saw melted her deathbed bravado.

"When will I get to hold this beautiful child?" she asked.

How, my heart asked, does the beloved become despised and then beloved again? I'd brought my dear Olivia, whom my mother could hold only as a life-sized paper image, while she brought her broken heart out from its longtime hiding place. Her arms were open too. She knew she would be leaving soon. "I'm ready for Jesus to come for me," she said.

I bent to kiss her good-bye. I could hear someone playing a recorder down the hall, a carol in a minor key. I waved to her from the door. She waved back. Over her shoulder, through the window, I could see the snow falling, like peace, onto the hospital parking lot.

# Uncreated Light

fter estimating that my time assignment for the New Testament class would take more than twenty hours to complete, I arranged for Reverend Frank to cover for me at my student church. The Friday afternoon of my arrival, Drew's campus was nearly empty and the day students' dormitory room, all mine. By evening, I had fallen into a rhythm of work and rest. I felt no pressure. My recreation comprised of jogging to the cafeteria and, after eating, a brisk walk around campus.

By Saturday afternoon, I'd logged fifteen hours of identifying and labeling sources for the gospel of Luke. Surprisingly, the exercise had become much more than selecting my choices and writing them down in my neatest italic. Word by word, phrase by phrase, I was introduced to Luke's congregation and to Luke's Jesus. For me, his gospel seems, still, to contain more compelling detail than the other three.

Around four o'clock, the sky began to cloud over. I turned

on the desk lamp. A mist had formed on the outside of the windowpanes. If rain was in the offing, something had put a hold on it. Minutes later, the entire room became completely dark. Blackness filled the window frames like square patches of velvet. The windows looking out on this sudden night scene were partly open, letting in the moist sweet air of early spring.

Immersed in this new darkness, I blinked a few times. I felt relaxed yet alert. In the narrow beam of light coming from my desk lamp, I could see outlines of the furniture in the room. Outside, however, darkness covered everything like a total eclipse. Yet, unlike a total eclipse, the darkness didn't come on gradually but all at once. I remained seated at my desk, trying to sort out the unexplainable—a freak storm without wind or rain; a daytime blackout.

All at once, a great light entered the room. Not a blinding light like the sun's, but a round, substantive light. The sky outside my windows remained dark. As for my poor desk lamp, it was completely drowned out by the greater light. I stayed quiet in my chair while I watched the illumination transform everything—my books, the walls, my water glass. Each object shimmered and came alive. Colors flowed into one another, glowing yet not changing the forms of things. There existed no way to measure the duration of this illumination. In what seemed like a short while, the greater light withdrew, and the gray afternoon came back into sight. That illumination seemed at that time and ever after to be a visit from God.

I'd never told anyone about this. Who would believe me?

There are many people who glimpse God's mysteries and have no one they trust enough to tell. Some, however, trust their pastor enough, and that is how I know.

# The Man Who Played Jesus

"**Y**ou've got to bring it up from your gut!" Ron yelled, jumping down from the stage at the back of the sanctuary. He stood facing us, one hand over his solar plexus and his face turning red with rage. "Here, like this: 'Crucify him! Crucify him!'" His voice echoed chillingly throughout the cavernous space.

Ron, a member of my congregation, had auditioned for and won the part of Jesus during our local churches' endeavor to stage a Passion play. Because of his directing experience, Ron was asked to assist with play's direction as well. He told us that if we held back our passion we'd obscure the Gospel's message, and if we didn't accurately demonstrate the call for violence against Jesus following his arrest, people might not recognize the need to fight against violence everywhere.

The other cast members and I needed to hear these admonitions from Ron because he was the surrogate recipient of our feigned hatred. We watched as a group of actors pretended to flog Ron, and we listened as nails were hammered into wood planks backstage, simulating the sounds of someone being crucified. Before each performance, Ron advised us all to check our egos at the door. The most important thing, he said, was to make this event seem as if it were happening now.

The efforts of Saint Sebastian Roman Catholic Church to organize the play drew involvement and support from area clergy and their several congregations. After making a critical examination of the script, the planning committee asked an area rabbi to read it, to ensure that it was free from prejudice against the Jewish people.

Parishioners from neighboring churches volunteered to act and sing in the play. During its three-year run, rehearsals and performances were held at Saint Sebastian's. I sang and acted with the choir/angry mob. Our voices consistently failed to reach a blood-curdling volume during rehearsals, but at the Good Friday performances, although it made us sick at heart, we shouted "Crucify him!" with all our might, from the solar plexus.

On stage the choir stood close to the audience. The women wore long skirts and covered their heads with flowing shawls. The men wore dark robes they found in their church's choir closets and tied them around their waists with rope. During each performance we'd all step down from the stage and encourage the audience to shout or sing with us.

Jesus' mother wore faded blue and white like the plaster statues of Mary on front-lawn altars. The actress who played

Mary Magdalene wet her face from the church's water cooler before coming on stage so that her cheeks would appear tear-stained. Every year Magdalene wore a green velvet dress her church's quilt-makers sewed for the occasion. It didn't fit the era, but she looked so lovely standing on the stage, her eyes appropriately stricken, that no one said a thing.

By Easter morning, the Ron we all knew had returned—a smart, quirky guy who was always ready to make us laugh. I loved visiting his home, an exquisite garden space with plants everywhere—in windows, on floors, and hanging from the ceilings. Antiques and wonderful curios invited hands-on inspection. Not surprisingly, everyone in his family brimmed with talent. Ron's wife, Sue Anne, played piano and organ. Their two daughters studied piano and sang for our services and shows. Their son pursued the visual arts.

Freed from the pressure of the holidays, I'd go to their home on Sunday evenings after the day's services had ended. In the family room downstairs, I'd take off my shoes and recline in front of the TV on a fluffy white rug. Sue Anne would bring in a tray of cheese and crackers with cold cuts and sliced apples, and she'd sit on the couch while Ron sat in his big recliner near the window. Every week, Ron recorded videos of the funniest comedians on TV, ensuring a much-needed hour or two of helpless laughter.

As an actor, Ron couldn't be typecast in a role. In real life he played many parts, as well: husband, father, church lay leader, advocate for AIDS patients, stage director, and antique collector. If there was anything that might have been incongruous with his yearly portrayal of Jesus, it was his job as financial consultant for a munitions plant. Overseeing the business side of making bombs and assault rifles is a far cry from providing companionship for men dying of AIDS—or, in the case of Jesus, healing the sick and raising the dead. Although his spiritual preparation for the role was invisible and unknowable perhaps even to him, I saw no harm in his trying to be more like Jesus.

Ron's preparation for his role in the Passion play kept him busy from late winter to early spring. Around the time the groundhog was making his appearance in Punxsutawney, Pennsylvania, Ron was thinking about his role as Jesus in northwest New Jersey. The first part of his transformation was physical as he grew his reddish-brown hair down to his shoulders. During Holy Week, while Ron labored over his performance, I labored over my sermon. Every Easter, I attempted to see with a child's eye what the disciples present on that day could hardly grasp: how ultimate humiliation could lead to ultimate glory. All that week Ron was alone with his thoughts, just as I was with mine. Sue Anne rehearsed the music for the upcoming services while their children enjoyed time with their friends and looked forward to a break from school.

Ron's inward journey remained a mystery. He never spoke about it to me or, as far as I knew, to anyone else. It wasn't until after the third annual performance that he showed any sign of negative stress. I admit that I often wondered about the last scene in the play, where he took off his robe and appeared in a loin cloth on the way to be "crucified." Members of the cast said they felt a sense of shock during that scene, even though we'd seen it in rehearsals more than once. Ron would stand near the front of the stage as his fellow actors simulated nailing him to the cross. It didn't matter that the blood was really catsup or that his crown of thorns was made of twigs that fell from the trees in the churchyard. The image of this nearly naked Jesus brought to mind those huge sculpted crucifixes in the hallways of Catholic hospitals. This corpus, however, wasn't made of wood or marble but of flesh. Ron's body, though moderately muscular, looked so incredibly soft, so open to wounding.

Some nights before going to bed, I'd imagine Ron propped up against the cross, the watered-down catsup trickling from his hands and his side. A sixteen-year-old who played the role of a soldier had filled a balloon with water and fastened it to Ron's waist. He engineered it in such a way that, when punctured, a stream of water poured down his side and mixed with the "blood," creating a pleural effusion just as John's Gospel describes.[4] ("The water was always cold as ice," Ron told me.)

Mesmerized, we all watched in awe of Ron's seemingly inborn genius as he depicted Jesus in these critical moments. How was he able to convey the Lord's despair so effectively? His crying out of Jesus' last words on the cross—"My God,

---

[4] Jn 19:34

my God, why have you forsaken me?"[5]—made me want to ask him if he'd ever been cruelly treated as a child or young adult. I couldn't help but wonder.

During the crucifixion scene, women from the Orthodox churches wept aloud. Some of them crept up to the edge of the stage and tried to touch Ron's feet before two young actors wrapped him in a white sheet and carried him offstage. It didn't occur to me until the night his anxiety broke through his mask of self-control how severely such an intense response from the people may have shaken him.

The night after our third annual Good Friday play, Ron and Sue Anne invited me to go with them and their children to see a performance on the outskirts of New York City.

"Let's see how we compare to the professionals," Ron joked.

We had only a couple of hours to recover from the performance that afternoon before we made our way into the city. We adults didn't talk much on the way, but Ron and Sue Anne's two daughters, who were sitting next to me in the back seat, kept up their soft magpie-like exchange.

The theater filled quickly for the eight o'clock show. Glued to our seats, we watched what seemed a caricature of our efforts at Saint Sebastian's earlier in the day. From where we were sitting, the actors resembled animated miniatures. Their voices were more suited for a British drama than for a story set in old Jerusalem. Pontius Pilate was suitably cowardly and Jesus

---

[5] Mk 15:34, NRSV

suitably holy, but not one of the actors was someone we knew or might come to know.

After the crucifixion scene, we heard grinding noises coming from the stage. The stagehands had engineered an extravagant Ascension, the biblical event where Jesus, after making many post-resurrection appearances to his disciples, is taken, bodily, up into heaven. In light of church tradition that places the Ascension forty days after the crucifixion; putting these two events so close together was a major error. The most holy of men, tortured and killed only minutes before, suddenly reappears floating in the air fully clothed? I suspect the play's writer or director wanted a happy ending. If no understudy stood in for Jesus, the actor who played the part would have to get dressed and made up, and be attached to wire rigging before being hoisted through the steamy clouds. Beams of light with the intensity of approximately 200 watts illuminated his travel upward. Robustly alive and wearing a flowing red coat, this unrecognizable Jesus seemed a mockery. Looking sideways at Ron's family, I saw three faces looking sideways at me while Ron held his head in his hands.

Escaping the theater seemed an act of deliverance. As I settled into the car for the drive home, one of the girls leaned her head against the window and fell asleep while the other drifted onto my shoulder. We had moved beyond the heaviest traffic when Ron began to speak.

"I think I saw myself tonight," Ron said, enunciating each word slowly, the way one might speak when hearing one's own voice over a microphone. "It was pretty hard to take. There I was, practically naked, *pretending* to be Jesus." He put weight on the word *pretending* as though ridiculing himself. "What could be stupider than that?"

Sue Anne turned around to see if the girls had heard him. The elder sister stirred against my arm before settling back into sleep. Unable to think of a response, neither of us spoke.

"I saw myself," Ron exclaimed. "Myself!" he repeated. A sob wrenched his throat. He stopped speaking for a while. Tears streamed down the side of his cheek. He brushed them away like a boy trying to be brave.

After a few minutes, Ron began to laugh, as though he were trying to slough off his meandering words, but his laugher lasted too long and had an anxious edge. It was scary to see him behave so strangely while driving us down the highway late at night.

Sue Anne turned around again to check on the girls. Then, she put her hand firmly on Ron's thigh, as if to ground him in the present and to call him back to a safer place. Her grounding intervention didn't work. He began to speak again, taking great gasps of breath between phrases.

"Just think. I saw myself just like I was not real. *He*—Jesus—was real, but not me. I mean *the* Jesus—the Christ—of course. Not that stupid actor."

He began to cry again and continued to repeat, "I am not real!" He let himself sob more freely until he began to laugh again. This laughter accompanied by tears alarmed me. His wet right cheek reflected the oncoming traffic lights.

Sue Anne shifted her whole body closer to his, as though intending to take the wheel, but, stopped short. I held my breath, fearing that Ron might turn into a wild man, someone we wouldn't recognize. Sue Anne shouted for Ron to pull over to the side of the road. He obeyed. Finding a small paper bag in the glove compartment, she told him to breathe into it. That broke the spell. After sighing loudly a few times, he quieted down.

"Well," he said, in his normal voice, "what do you think of that?" as though he had been outside himself the whole time, just acting, looking on. How like him to attempt to disguise his temporary crack-up with a show of aplomb.

We neared home. Both girls woke at the sound of the stones crunching under the wheels in my driveway as Ron braked to let me out. I went to bed figuring that he would sleep it off. He'd cut his hair and maybe feel shaky for a day or two. In a couple of days, he'd be his old self.

Ron did cut off what we'd come to call his "Jesus hair;" but the next day Sue Anne took him to the mental health clinic because he couldn't sleep or stop talking. At first, the psychiatrist thought Ron was going through a manic phase, but since he'd reached middle age without a single manic episode, he was treated for reactive depression, a run-of-the-mill diagnosis with expectation of a full recovery. In a few months Ron's depression lifted. That spring, the Bishop's Cabinet appointed me to another congregation.

Many years have passed. Ron and Sue Anne, with a handful

of other people, still care for that little church down the road. The current pastor and her husband are much loved. Newer ministries include a soup kitchen in a neighboring city and the crocheting of hundreds of prayer shawls as gifts for people sick or in trouble. Thanks to Sue Anne and the new pastor's husband, a fine tenor, the church continues to enjoy wonderful music. Ron still acts in local theater productions and serves regularly as a liturgist on Sunday mornings.

Usually, the miracle of human transformation isn't instantaneous. Maybe the ego must shatter for a new spirit to take shape. And maybe we need to gain another perspective on our perceived incompetence. What better outcome of a crack-up than to make friends with our own humanity. Ron, in his effort to see and feel who Jesus really was and is, discovered who he, himself, really was and is. I mean Ron in the robe and prickly crown; Ron in the loincloth; Ron wrapped in the white sheet from head to toe; and, yes, Ron, in the car that night driving us back from the stage production near the city.

Ron agrees that he began to get at the truth of his experience the moment he began to laugh and cry at the same time. His grieving for his imperfect self was invaded by a stroke of awareness. His sorrow got all tangled up with his joy in this existence, which offers us another chance, and then another, until, at last, Christ offers us yet one more—the chance to weep and rejoice beyond decrepitude. Yes, even beyond death itself.

# Carlos

At the sound of seat belts being fastened, I felt indescribable relief. We had just boarded a plane from Miami to New York. I'd claimed my aisle seat over the wing, while Jenny had reserved the bulkhead seat toward the front. Following ten days together on a boat, we had no need to talk. About a month earlier, Jenny, a swimming buddy and new member of one of my churches, had shown me an advertisement for a scuba diving cruise and persuaded me to sign up. It was a bargain, she said, at less than one hundred dollars a day.

We were a group of fourteen, counting the cruise's captain and galley cook. The forty-five-foot recycled barge had been rigged with a mast and sails. On the night of our stormy crossing, its four huge propellers pushed us over the ocean toward the islands. The captain assigned us, in pairs, to take spells at the wheel while he slept. The next morning, the deck looked like laundry day in the barrio with all our rain-soaked clothing hanging out to dry.

Caribbean waters are lovely and warm, but I never found the courage to tumble in with an oxygen tank on my back. Even during the required scuba diving class, I balked at the heavy equipment and wouldn't wear flippers. So, while Jen and the other guests, who were mostly male, took photos of shark's teeth and coral reefs, my days were spent on deck reading paperbacks and acquiring a deep, probably dangerous, tan. My snorkeling occurred only with the boat anchored close to shore. After making the best of it, I was ready to go home.

Chocolate I'd bought during a bus trip around St. Maarten, a cold raspberry yogurt, and a new paperback—all of which I'd stowed in my smaller carry-on bag—ensured a pleasurable flight. The couple in the adjoining seats seemed nice enough, but their little granddaughter, who was sitting with her parents behind us, chattered and sang nonstop. Eventually, I told myself, she'd grow tired and fall asleep.

I had just settled in when a young flight attendant stopped to check my ticket stub and ask my name.

"Your friend said you were an EMT," he began. *Jenny must have told him that,* I thought, annoyed.

"My certification has expired," I said.

"We have a baby on his way to New York for surgery. His transport couldn't make it. The captain asked if you could take care of him."

Legal liability came to mind. I'd been warned during first-aid training about the dangers of giving emergency care in public places.

"How sick is the baby?" I asked.

"He's not sick," the young man began defensively. "The surgery is . . . corrective." He frowned, seemingly, at the responsibility of securing my agreement. "The baby is already here," he said, "on the plane." Anxiety kept him talking. "He's fine, actually. He just needs someone to take care of him during the flight. You know, we want to make sure the person is— has some skills. The stewardess, she could bring him to you. I mean, now, right away, in a New York minute!"

*An oddly persuasive soliloquy,* I thought. Maybe he was worried that my refusal might delay takeoff. I hesitated, trying to assess the situation. If the baby wasn't ill, there shouldn't be a problem.

"Okay," I said.

Looking relieved, the attendant took the canvas diaper bag off his shoulder, put it on my lap, and disappeared behind the first-class curtain. I unzipped the bag to find predictable contents: a bottle of formula, diapers, a quilted pad, sterile wipes, and tissues. The tiny white undershirt in a clear plastic envelope would fit a baby less than two months old. Only the eye dropper offered a bit of mystery.

A female flight attendant walked toward me carrying the infant wrapped in a blue blanket. She placed the bundle in my arms. Only his eyes were showing.

"His name is Carlos," she said. "Call if you need anything."

Eager to see his face, I turned my body as far as I could toward the aisle before lifting the corner of the blanket. The terrible empty hollow beneath his eyes increased my caution. Part of one nostril was missing, and there was a gaping hole where his mouth should have been. I peered into the esophageal opening. Even his chin had lost definition from an extreme cleft palate. I hid his face by carefully folding back the blanket in such a way that it wouldn't interfere with his breathing.

As soon as we were airborne, the older couple in the adjoining seats began to confer in whispers. The wife leaned over and spoke to me, conspiringly.

"I hope you don't mind," she said, "but we're going to ask the stewardess to move you." Her husband pointed at Carlos and added, "*It* might frighten our granddaughter."

I felt as though someone had referred to my own child as *it*. Moreover, I'd caught the man in a lie. His granddaughter surely had gotten a thorough look. The moment Carlos, all funneled in blue, was placed in my arms, her sing-song vocalizations stopped. As for being frightened, she showed no sign of fear. The entire time she remained leaning over the back of my seat, breathing her peppermint breath against my neck. Shortly after the child's grandfather pushed the call button, the female attendant who'd brought Carlos to me came walking toward us. Unfazed by my seatmates' request, she smiled at them and led me to the back of the plane.

A row of empty seats afforded me privacy and room to move around. I was able to lay Carlos across my lap and rest my left arm against the window ledge. It was easy, while holding him, to lean back against the window frame and pull up my knees over the empty seats. Relaxing into our new setting, I was glad for having no reason to hide his face. I watched Carlos wake and sleep. He took shallow, wispy breaths and opened his eyes to look up at me. When he coughed, saliva spilled into his ear from the corner of his cheekbone. I blotted it with a sterile cotton pad. When I changed his diaper, I was grateful to see his little legs energetically kicking the air and his genitals intact.

Holding Carlos, I gazed down at his fragile form and wondered what The Eternal One might feel while looking down on any of us who are stripped of beauty and function, and with what ought to be found only under our skin—strands of raw muscle and a wet pulsing glottis in this baby's case—left exposed to every curious eye. It must be true about God loving the ragtag people better than those of us who fit within the norms of function and appearance.

The warmth of this child's body against mine brought the same sweet comfort that my infant son's brought years ago. What shook me then shook me now—my depth of longing for this child's safety, for his life. As Carlos lay awake, I looked down into his intelligent eyes and softly spoke my thoughts:

"Carlos," I said, "when the surgeon gives you your new face, you'll have a mouth and cheeks like most other children. Your cry will have a shape. Surely the surgeon has helped other babies like you and given them a better chance to live and to grow." I almost added "and to be loved." Chilled by my accidental blunder, I shut up for a while. Didn't I love him now? Didn't his mother love him enough to hand him over, trembling, to strangers on this flying machine? There was relief in my conclusion. Leaning over close to Carlos, I whispered, "Your mother loves you very, very much."

For babies like Carlos, surgery is a necessity to enable the basics of breathing and eating. The surgery would also help to prevent kids in the school yard and people like my former seatmates from recoiling at the sight of him.

How is it, I asked myself, that I feel no revulsion, no fear, while flying through the clouds with Carlos at 400 miles an hour? How is it that, while holding him in my arms and looking into his un-resurrected face, I feel only a sinking love? How is it that when I fill an eyedropper with formula and feed Carlos drop by drop, as though he were a small bird in peril, I can breathe normally and envision his eventual healing? How is it that when I say his name, the strangely solitary "Carlos," I feel as though we are truly family to one another?

There were lighter moments to balance the meditative ones. A few passengers on their way to the restroom and flight attendants with carts of snacks and soda turned to smile and say hello to Carlos and me. After a week in the sun, the color of my skin matched his exactly. Aware that a medical emergency could arise during the flight, I offered thanks for each uneventful hour. Carlos could have aspirated the formula and asphyxiated, or, given his handicap and the fact that he was separated from his mother while in a pressurized cabin for hours, he could have died from coronary shock. Gratitude for our peaceful time together led to sadness about our inevitable parting.

Although my ears hurt as we lost altitude, the lessening of cabin pressure didn't seem to bother Carlos. But the churning city that was rising up to meet us, the lowering of the plane's landing gear, and the whirring of the reversed jet engines reminded me of his vulnerability. He was on his way to a hospital for surgery and to a new life. Now I was the one who must let him go.

As the plane landed, Carlos stirred peacefully awake. His dark eyes glowed. I had fed and changed him again. Brown and skinny in his new white shirt, he was ready to be given to the medical transport personnel waiting at the gate. As the other passengers slowly exited from the plane, I remained seated until the steward motioned for me to come forward. I carried Carlos, my treasure, past the empty seats to the exit. We were last.

I recognized the hospital's transport team immediately, noting the EMT's emblem on his front pocket and the nurse's photo ID hanging from a cord around her neck. I stood facing them with the baby wrapped in his blue blanket with only his eyes visible, just as I'd received him.

"Is this Carlos?" the nurse asked kindly, knowing, of course, that it was.

"This is Carlos," I answered, and handed him over. They thanked me.

"Don't mention it," I said, stumbling toward Jenny, who waited near the edge of the crowd with our carry-on bags. From the airport we took a shuttle to Port Authority. During the two-hour bus trip home, we ate our stash of Dutch chocolate and dozed off.

In the following weeks, I entertained clergy and church friends with anecdotes from my vacation. I told them about the storm on the way over and our crazy captain. I confessed my cowardice about diving with scuba equipment. I explained that, with basic snorkel gear, I was able to see a school of yellow fish that looked like a flock of canaries and a sea horse swimming sideways.

I didn't tell them that I had seen what no one else had seen deep in the underworld of God's creation, or that I had fallen for a baby who was missing half his face. In this little child I recognized the utter helplessness of being. There are events between birth and death that could make any one of us dependent upon whoever happens to be near.

Let the stranger by your side, and mine, always be a loving witness to the terrifying universe within—and without.

# Elmer Rising

I first met Elmer early on a Thanksgiving morning when he was a patient in critical care. He was comatose, immobilized by tubes, and his skin had turned dark yellow. Thea, his wife, had called me the night before.

"I know it's a holiday weekend," she said, her voice wispy, birdlike, "but would you go and pray with him? The doctor said it would be soon, within a few days. My husband didn't go to church, but he was a believer."

Thea blended in so well with the congregation's white-haired widows that I never knew she had a husband until her phone call. I told her I would go first thing in the morning.

The hospital was en route to my sister's house, where family and friends would be gathering for the holiday feast. The dusty odor from potted mums in the back seat of my car made me sneeze. Between sneezes, I laughed at myself. Although allergic to mums, I persist in buying them as gifts year after year. For me, Thanksgiving, purple mums, and Advent belong together.

Having never met Elmer, I wondered how he might receive me. As I stood outside his door, I silently prayed this ancient prayer several times before entering his room, "Lord Jesus Christ, son of God, have mercy on me, a sinner."[6] Initially, as a student pastor, I had some shyness in asking for mercy and some embarrassment in calling myself a sinner, but, over the years, I've noticed how well this prepared me for the difficult things I saw and heard in home and hospital settings.

As I approached Elmer, I could tell his breaths were uneven and too far apart. His eyes were shut as though sealed, and his lids were leathery. I pulled a chair close to his bed and sat down.

"Elmer?" I said and then introduced myself as Thea's pastor. Since hearing is believed to be the last sense to go when a person's dying, I continued as though Elmer could hear me. "I hope it's okay. I came to say a prayer with you."

Elmer showed no sign of awareness. His hand in mine was dry and hard as wood—a carved balsam hand, cold to the touch. I spoke the words that came to me in times like this, beginning by thanking God for the love that has followed us down through the years, and then asking the Holy Spirit to quiet our hearts and bring us to a place of assurance. For death-bed prayers, as with Elmer, I offered a reminder of Jesus' promise to prepare a place for us in heaven. I paused a lot to give the sick person the chance to fill the spaces with words or thoughts of his or her own. Toward the end, I'd say the

---

6 "The Jesus Prayer," from ancient Christian Orthodox tradition

Lord's Prayer.[7] I've learned to watch patients' lips. People with dementia and even people in a coma often remember the words they'd learned as a child, but Elmer's lips did not move.

I stood up, but having been there for less than five minutes I didn't feel right about leaving. The day ahead would be full of distractions. For now, there was no need to hurry. I pulled my chair closer to the window. The early sun drew me into its warmth. I would stay with Elmer for a while, honoring my promise to Thea. There's no formula for such companioning, no map. We couldn't talk, so I sat there, taking in the warm sunlight and calling on God in my heart—although not so much calling as entreating God that Elmer be watched over, loved.

During our time together I never saw another soul. No one came to the door. No one asked who I was. On my way out, I passed so near the nurses' station that I could smell the coffee from their paper cups on the countertop. Several nurses sat before piles of charts, but not one of them looked up. I had been an invisible visitor to a patient without hope.

Thanksgiving at my sister's was a mostly pleasant vacation from my everyday life. There was, predictably, too much food and too much conversation with a little indigestion from each. Asked to say a blessing over our meal, I later became a sounding board for guests. The busy social environment distanced me from Elmer's suffering. My head cleared as I got out into the fresh air and onto the highway heading north, able at last to

---

[7] Mt 6:9–15

settle back into who I am. After three hours on the road, I
turned into the driveway and unlocked the front door, thankful
to be home.

I dropped my bags in the living room and went directly to
the blinking answering machine, certain that there would be
news of Elmer's death.

"… took a turn for the better," I heard Thea saying, her
voice sounding stronger than it did two days ago. "I want to
tell you something," she continued. "Elmer told me not to tell
anyone, and I don't know what to make of it." I turned up the
volume so that I didn't miss a word. "Elmer said Jesus came
and told him it wasn't his time yet. Now, everyone knows my
husband isn't religious. He's afraid if this gets out people will
think he's crazy."

I called her right back. Thea told me about Elmer's medical
improvement, and I asked about his state of mind.

"Well," Thea stalled, "he didn't say anything else unusual,
and he's so much better. Yesterday he was at death's door, and
now he's coming home, maybe tomorrow."

"Tomorrow?"

"The doctor said tomorrow or Monday; it depends. He
has to keep the feeding tube in for good, you know." Another
pause. "Maybe you could stop by the house sometime next
week?"

When I arrived at their home, I was struck by how tiny it
was. The whole street was lined with small, well-kept houses,
their mini-lawns all neatly trimmed. I felt freakishly tall

walking along the concrete path to the front door of what may have been the smallest house on the block. My two-story parsonage was four times its size.

I rang the doorbell. Thea answered, smiling broadly. When I reached out to her, she held up her hands to hold me off. Her palms were covered with flour.

"We're making donuts!" she exclaimed with laughter in her voice.

Looking down the hallway past Thea, I could see Elmer standing at the entrance of the kitchen, watching us. Both of them wore long white bakers' aprons. Elmer's face beamed under smears of flour. At his waist his feeding tube made a slight protrusion.

"Yes," he said, "come in. We're having a great time!"

I followed Thea into the kitchen, which smelled of sugar and hot oil. There was an incongruity about them making donuts since, thanks to his feeding tube, Elmer couldn't have more than a taste, and I didn't know what to say at first. I grinned before taking a breath and blurting out my banality.

"How wonderful you're so much better!"

Elmer wiped his right hand on his apron and reached out to shake mine. The closer I stood to them, the more of a giant I became, a self-conscious five foot, ten inches, against their less-than five feet. Elmer held on to my hand for a moment with both of his. His face turned serious.

"Thea told you what happened on Thanksgiving," he confided softly. "No one else has to know, right?"

"No one else has to know." I answered.

An incredulous guest, I watched them as they covered up the dough, turned off the deep fryer, took off their aprons, and washed their hands. They led me into a tiny parlor off the kitchen that contained an easy chair and a love seat. One window opened onto a green willow tree, which kept me from feeling claustrophobic. I sat on the love seat beside Thea, and Elmer lowered himself onto the chair. Our feet—their four very little ones and my two very big ones—took up most of the space in the middle of the small room. While I sat next to Thea, I got used to the homey cubical. She spoke realistically about Elmer's temporary recovery, saying he may live a few months more at most.

"I'm glad for the extra time," Elmer said. "I'll have Christmas and maybe my birthday."

I then said a prayer that acknowledged their thankfulness and ended with the Lord's Prayer. This time Elmer was able to participate, and the size of the room made it possible for us to hold hands in a circle without reaching or straining. After we finished, Elmer told me briefly about his life, focusing mostly on hard work and family. He and Thea had children and grandchildren in the area. I wondered how two kids had grown to adulthood in this dollhouse of a dwelling and how they found room for relatives at holiday meals.

Before I left, I offered to visit every week. Our visits spanned a period of three months and were roughly a half hour each time. We usually sat in the living room—Elmer on the couch, me in the chair. Thea stayed in the background so that Elmer and I could have uninterrupted time together. Emerging from some corner of the house, she'd join us for a few minutes before I left.

One day I saw canvas boards stacked against the living room wall. Someone had brought oil paintings—Elmer's handiwork—up from the basement. Providing little commentary, Elmer let me look through them. They were quite good, actually, revealing the shapes of clouds and trees in different seasons. His reticence suggested he'd kept his painting a secret. I thought of the solitary hours he must have spent with brush in hand, painting all those trees, leaf by leaf. I wondered if he feared that his practice of art, itself a form of holiness, would cause some awkwardness among his friends.

When Christmas arrived, it was everything Elmer had hoped for. His family was close enough to touch, and one of his grandchildren gleefully tore open presents. I continued to visit him through the New Year, learning something new about him every time—his observations about the world, and his growing faith, which seemed to be at the core of his hesitant but engaging manner. I became as easy with Elmer as with an old friend. I could visit him while wearing jeans and a baggy sweater, unless I was on my way to the hospital, which required my wearing a clerical collar. Elmer and I laughed together often. We admired the snow falling and the wind blowing. Toward the end, we marveled at the warmth of a late February day that seemed to herald spring's early arrival.

Elmer succeeded in achieving something that's so difficult for most of us: moment-by-moment awareness. He was grateful he had no pain. When I asked him about his encounter with Jesus, he gave me the same answer he'd given Thea. "I just don't want anyone to think I'm a crazy guy," he said, looking at the floor.

Elmer made it through the winter. The warning call came shortly after his birthday.

"The doctor was just here and said he could go this week," Thea told me. A faint wail cut through her sigh.

I went over right away to sit with them. Elmer had grown thinner over the past few weeks, but his face still had color, and he conversed with the same quiet cheerfulness that he had throughout his reprieve. "Tomorrow," he said, "I'm going to call my sister and say goodbye." His sister lived in another state and was unable to travel.

The next morning Elmer called his sister. They talked for a long time. The afternoon of the following day when I had just finished washing my hair, Elmer's son called to say his father had died. With wet hair and wearing jeans, I got into my car and was at Elmer's home in a flash. Three generations of family filled the living room. The adults were on chairs arranged in a tight semicircle with small children sitting on the floor.

Elmer's blue-pajama-clad body sat like a statue in his usual spot, one arm resting along the back of the couch. His face still had some color. His eyes were open and bluer than ever in the afternoon light. He resembled a figure in a Renaissance painting, a saint in prayer or an angel staring heavenward. But this was no imitation of fifteenth-century art.

I tried to pay attention to Elmer's daughter telling me how he died—how they were sitting there, having a conversation, when he took his last breath; how there was no gasp, no struggle, but my attention kept returning to Elmer. His abandoned body told a story of its own.

When two men from the funeral home arrived, we were all sent into the other rooms, but Elmer's daughter insisted on remaining with the men to ensure that everything was done right. I stayed with Thea. We leaned against the kitchen door, listening to her daughter direct the men as they put Elmer's body on a wheeled stretcher.

"Don't close his eyes!" we heard her say. "He always slept with his eyes open."

Thea started to cry. I put my arm around her.

My thoughts went back to that Thanksgiving morning in the hospital, when Elmer's eyes were shut so tight that his lashes seemed to be glued to his cheeks. I'm certain that, upon waking, he realized his good fortune of being given time for catching up with his soul. Elmer left us with a memory more durable than any photograph, sitting in those blue pajamas, his eyes open wide as though looking toward his welcome.

I still sigh for Elmer—a kind and simple man, a baker of donuts who could no longer relish the crisp dough's sweetness, an artist who hid his work away, a late disciple who heard and, perhaps, saw the Lord and kept silent in his rejoicing.

# Pauline's Fire

Four-year-old Pauline, who sat very quietly and attentively during Sunday services, had become a precocious presence in my congregation. She reminded me of my early devotion to God during the year I lived in the convent school.

On weekdays I would see her playing in the grass near the driveway of my big stone parsonage. Her family lived next door, and our backyards were separated by a line visible only to surveyors. When I'd speak to Pauline, she'd usually look up at me slowly, her eyes locking with mine. Other times she'd say hi while keeping her eyes on a toy in the grass. I identified with her extraordinary shyness, even though by then I'd become more comfortable with smiling and greeting people as part of my pastor's role.

On Pentecost Sunday, Pauline's family was sitting where they always sat, near the entrance of a pew two-thirds of the way back. There were more than a handful of children in the congregation that day, thanks to the worship committee. Its members convinced me that "Birthday of the Church" was a more child-friendly than the word "Pentecost," which can get lost in translation. A few women baked and decorated birthday cakes that we would finish off during coffee hour.

Twenty red helium-filled balloons broke the solemnity of the colonial-style sanctuary. They rose from strings tied to radiators along the walls and from the balcony's railings. Through the sea of benched pews, I could see the red ties and scarves and jackets of parishioners. They wore red to celebrate the holy fire, those flames of Spirit the Book of Acts tells us appeared above the heads of believers during Pentecost.

Watching the sanctuary fill with people, an unholy fire burned inside me. Adam and I had met at a conference in the Midwest for church pastors. During the three-week stay dedicated to studying scripture, I fell in love with him. We sat together in class and during meals. We talked for hours. While Adam drew a clear boundary between friendship and romance, my emotions flowed like a river in a rain storm. It was hopeless from the beginning. He'd lived in a world of alcohol addiction and troubled relationships, and regardless of his new sobriety, he was still unhappy. Even though he'd stopped drinking, during the past year his wife had moved with their children to another town.

There was no chance for the two of us to develop even a slow friendship, since he lived a thousand miles away. At the end of our few companionable weeks, the relationship was over for him. For me, however, our parting brought a disproportionate sense of loss.

Work became my balm in Gilead. My stomach got nervous and upset only when empty and when I wasn't busy, so I ate frequently and scheduled myself severely. My ministry held me together. While Sunday services brought additional pressure because I was so visible, keeping focused on my message carried me through.

After adjusting the light on the lectern during the Pentecost service, I lowered myself onto the tall ornately carved mahogany chair and breathed deeply. My breathing exercise took me from the prelude to the scripture readings. By then, I'd breathed myself into clearer consciousness. I read aloud the Ezekiel passage about the valley of dry bones, about how God's directed prophesy would take those old bones from their first rattling to the formation of human skeletons. Moving forward, the Great Spirit would flesh them out, breathe into them, and resurrect the people of Israel. God's intention, I believe, is to save us all from the graves of our hearts.[8]

"Hear the word of the Lord," I said with confidence, "as it comes to us on this Pentecost morning." Prepared to preach from memory, I stepped away from the pulpit to get closer to my parishioners.

All week long I'd spent time charting my message, shaping it to build expectation. Looking out over the congregation, I

[8] Ez 37:1–14

noticed Pauline creating a small disturbance. She was trying to get past her mother to exit the pew. Her mother whispered something into her ear while holding onto the child's shoulder to keep her seated. When her father cupped his hand over Pauline's other shoulder, she appeared barricaded from both sides. It unsettled me to see this shy child suffer any form of restraint. Her parents seemed to be trying to curb some childish impulse. This puzzled me, as they had always seemed so easygoing with her.

It was finally time to deliver my message, and I couldn't get the first word out. Almost a minute had passed since I'd read the scripture and been struck mute. My stomach felt like a hollow drum. The duration of this unexpected silence led the congregation to start coughing and rustling their bulletins. If this mad freeze lasted much longer, I could hardly proclaim the Spirit's coming, and no one would ever imagine those dry bones coming to life.

The people to my right had begun to whisper to one another. On my left, those closer to Pauline's family watched her struggle while shifting uncomfortably in their seats. Many parishioners seemed surprised, since they'd never seen Pauline even fidget during a service. Unlike other kids her age, she never took off to run around the sanctuary like a border collie. That Pentecost morning, I wished with all my heart she would.

Although practically immobilized, Pauline hadn't given up. She wrenched her body sharply to one side in an effort to loosen her parents' hold. Her face turned bright red. As she failed in her attempts to get away, I failed to redirect my attention. My eyes kept returning to the child, wondering what she wanted, what thwarted desire had caused her such desperation.

In my year at the convent school, I was passive and, as far as I know, offered no resistance to any rules. The school seemed a safe haven for a lost child. Pauline wasn't a lost child—and neither was I anymore, I reminded myself. Trying to regain a sense of control, I kept breathing deeply and evenly, hoping my anxiety would disappear and that I could begin my message and carry on. My mistake, I reasoned, had been to walk away from the pulpit, which put too much space between me and my notes. The reality, however, is that I was standing psychologically naked before my congregation. Pale Pauline—the quiet one, peaceful to a fault—had unexpectedly and thoroughly derailed my message. At the edge of Ezekiel's valley of dry bones, I faced my congregation with only one discernible thought: to set Pauline free.

I watched Pauline make one more sharp corkscrew turn and fail once again to get away. Intending to end the stalemate, I waved my hand and called out, "Let her go! Let her go!"

Caught off guard, her parents lifted their arms. Pauline sprang forward and exited the pew. Taking a moment to gather herself, she stood erect in the center of the aisle. Many in the congregation couldn't see her from where they sat because the backs of the wooden pews were an inch higher than her head. Her thin form moved slowly and deliberately down the aisle's gradual incline.

People stretched their bodies upward and sideways as they strained to witness this silent adventure. Some bent far over the edge of their seats to catch a glimpse of Pauline as she walked by; others raised themselves up by placing their hands on the back of the pew in front of them. Pauline, in her white dress on this warm May morning, was walking purposefully, as though she knew where she was going and why.

When she stood before me in the curve of the candlelit chancel, I went down on my knees to make us the same height. We were face-to-face, me in my white robe with the long red stole and Pauline in her white dress, her spirit aflame.

"What is it?" I asked, trying to speak softly because of the microphone clipped to my collar.

Pauline paused. She looked at me straight on with that locked-in gaze and then reached out her arms folding me into an embrace. Her thin chest pressed against my soft one. I put my arms around her, feeling the sharp bones of her shoulders.

Her eyes saw it all. In her watchfulness, Pauline had picked up on my pain. She broke through her shyness, fighting against her parents' reasonable boundaries, to show me a purer kind of love. I thought of Jesus promising his disciples that, after his leaving, he would send them the Holy Spirit as comforter.

Having been comforted, I saw at once that the romantic obsession pulling me down wasn't love at all. Admittedly, real love can be difficult to see. On that day, for instance, a number of people in the congregation, witnessing the embrace between a child and a pastor, let out sentimental sighs. Like so many of us, they missed the scope of love. The child got it, at least in that instant. But, really, there's no one who could begin to tell it.

The day's message survived this interruption. The dry bones of Ezekiel's valley rose up to take on flesh and hope, but the regaining of my thoughts and composure alone were not enough to send forth the Word. It took the Spirit's coming to us through a small child. It took Pauline's fight and Pauline's grace.

After the benediction, I stood in the doorway shaking hands and receiving hugs and unmerited compliments.

"You are amazing," a man said.

"God is amazing," I said. But what I wanted to say was: *Didn't you just see the Holy Spirit herself walking down the aisle?* That child showed us how the spirit of Christ requires our moving toward the sorrow we see in another person's being.

It's never easy for a person to change course, especially a child. How many of us have dared to struggle against authority in order to respond to another's needs? No matter how old we are, the secret of tending the spirit in us is to keep our child-self alive and strong.

By summer's end, I'd forgotten Adam, but I'll never forget the little girl who lived next door. Pentecost always brings her back. When I see the red balloons and listen to the hype about the Birthday of the Church, my thoughts take a serious turn. While thinking about ways I might help to make a better world for others, I have personal concerns as well. I must remember Pauline's fire for when my next loss comes.

# A Counseling Daughter

At age thirty, my counseling client Rosalie was nearly spherical in shape. Her business suits accentuated her girth, which undermined her impeccable style. I wondered how her weight might impact her work as a department store manager. Surely there were times when she needed to move around with some speed.

Rosalie's response to a question on her counseling intake form caught my eye: "Used to be Catholic. Do not want to talk about religion!" During the three years we met together on a weekly basis, she never did.

"All right if I call you Rosalie?" I asked at our first meeting.

"Well, that's my name," she answered, "but since my parents gave up on me they call me Rosa. At the store people call me Ms. Lopez."

When Rosalie shrugged her shoulders, no other part of her body moved. I found it difficult to suppress my fascination with her size.

"How old were you when your parents gave up on you?"

"Twelve," she said, "the year I got fat." Her face was impassive and her voice was calm, as though she were talking about someone else. "They took me to so many doctors. My mother gave me diets. Nothing helped."

Her parents' ambitions for their two daughters reflected their idea of the American Dream. They had emigrated from Puerto Rico before the girls were born and maintained their rule of not speaking Spanish at home. They also decided to give both of their girls English-sounding names. Caroline, who was five years older than Rosalie, got married right after her high school graduation and settled into family life. When Rosalie turned twenty, her parents paid for her to attend a local business school. Now, at thirty, single and friendless, she rented a small apartment near work.

Rosalie arrived in my office week after week modeling a seemingly endless supply of perfectly tailored suits—blouses buttoned up high around her throat, leather pumps and handbags in matching pastel colors. Pastels were her signature, pale blues, and pinks, and yellows, the colors of baby clothes.

At first, I almost bought the reason Rosalie gave for her lack of social ease. "If I were thin like my sister, Caroline, I would be a happier person, married by now and with kids," she said. While I believed that long-term counseling could lead to improved health and well-being for Rosalie, my colleagues were cautious about my optimistic prediction.

At the agency where I worked, we had weekly peer

supervision as well as one hour of individual supervision with a more advanced staff clinician. Two monthly meetings, one with a psychiatrist and one with a primary care physician, rounded out the in-house support all counselors received. I had private supervision also with a licensed psychologist. When I spoke to him about Rosalie, he warned me that my prejudgment of fat people could get in the way of my seeing and hearing her clearly.

From my perspective as a thin person, I saw fat people as undisciplined individuals who cared little for their health and appearance. Yet I saw how Rosalie took pains every day to present herself as close to her ideal of a professional woman as she possibly could, both in dress and in manner. Supervision taught me to avoid reacting to a client's appearance, words, or demeanor. It also taught me about the life-preserving instinct to sometimes overeat.

Among many species, accumulation of body fat is a function of staying alive in a dangerous world; eating is always better than not eating. More than one physician had suggested that I gain an extra ten pounds. An extra 100 pounds would have been an entirely different matter. In any event, I didn't want, either consciously or unconsciously, to convey rejection toward Rosalie or any other overweight person.

As a Hispanic child failing to model her parents' perfectionist ideals, Rosalie's shame reminded me a little of my father's. He was never able to celebrate being Italian. Regardless of the fact that he and others of our Genovese relatives were blond and blue-eyed, as well as successful in business and the professions, the cruel epithets used against Italian immigrants closed my father off. In the same way, being called Rosa closed Rosalie off. The diminutive not only reflected her parents' reduced expectations, but it contributed to her expressed self-image of being "nothing but a fat Puerto Rican girl."

In time I began to understand how Rosalie's layers of fashion and her layers of flesh protected her from what she perceived to be the world's dangers, especially intimacy. Rosalie spoke clearly and intelligently when expressing appreciation for the status she enjoyed at work. She admitted she had no idea how to begin a friendship and was a long way from her stated goal: to meet a man, have a family, and lead what she believed to be a normal life.

When I asked her to tell me about the boys and men she knew best, such as her father, cousins, or other relatives, she said, "They were just there. You know, watching ball games on TV. Blue-collar guys that didn't say much." Her mother stayed in the background, cooking and running the business of the house. During her childhood, Rosalie saw herself as striving to become a white-collar American and regarded her obesity as an irreversible handicap.

One afternoon, after a pause in our exchange, Rosalie took a deep breath and smoothed her skirt over her immense knees. "My uncle, Gustavo, lived next door," she said. "I'll tell you about him sometime." She didn't mention him again that week or the next.

Counselors follow the rule of restraint with clients they suspect have been sexually abused. We're trained never to initiate the subject or ask leading questions. After Rosalie mentioned her uncle, I decided to go in an entirely different direction and inquired about her girlfriends at school. She said the popular girls shunned her and that she didn't want to hang out with anyone who was depressed or fat—a curious but understandable response.

One day she asked: "Do you think it's possible for me to find a nice man?"

"Where do you go that you might meet someone?" I replied.

"Nowhere," she answered.

Rosalie's job kept her busy most weekdays. She confessed to being depressed on weekends and holiday breaks. She said she usually wore pajamas from Friday night though Sunday and seldom left her apartment. She had a pantry filled with cereal, popcorn, sweets, and other snacks. She ordered meals from restaurants, read magazines, watched movies, and planned her outfits for the coming week. Arriving at my office one day in pale blue from head to toe, she struck me as a large, round baby bird lost in a world that couldn't accommodate its needs.

Six months into her counseling, Rosalie began to tell me about the uncomfortable afternoons with her Uncle Gustavo. She described feelings of dread without giving specifics. I worked hard at staying patient while wondering why it would be so wrong to ask her plainly what happened.

A few weeks later, without warning, Rosalie became

consumed by a compelling distraction. She had begun to read the personals in the local newspaper and had spoken by phone with a handful of men who were looking for dates. With fatal innocence, she reported telling each one about being overweight, adding that she was "quite attractive and very neat." All true.

Until Herbert, each potential boyfriend declined a meeting. Herbert told her in their first phone call that he liked big women. His admission, which seemed to delight her, made me suspicious. From the photo she showed me, the short slight man looked uncomfortably self-conscious, His eyes seemed a bit shifty under his frowning, sweaty forehead.

"He has a good job at IBM," she said.

For some time, concern for Rosalie led me to feel anxious about how to be with her and what to say. I didn't say much, which is always better than saying too much or the wrong thing. Each week in supervision, I brought up my concerns. Colleagues told me not to try to be her mother and that I had no responsibility to protect her from her poor choices. When my in-house supervisor suggested I refer her to another counselor I got angry, claiming it was her relationship with Herbert that was getting on my nerves. My supervisor didn't buy it, and, to make things worse, Rosalie's conundrum of mysteries kept growing.

Over the next several months our sessions went from her providing a sad description of her first coffee-shop date with Herbert to her discussing the ways they were getting to know each other. This included dinners out, movies, and the tentative beginning of a physical relationship. Because of my concern about Rosalie possibility having been sexually abused by her uncle, I may have been too cautious with her for too long while trying to always come up with the most therapeutic questions. My suspicion about Rosalie's experience increased anytime she'd quickly skip over a reference to her Uncle Gustavo. At times I felt drawn against my will toward certain thoughts about Herbert. Although I never shared this imagination with my supervisors, Herbert and Gustavo had blended into one personality.

Eventually Rosalie and Herbert decided to get married. When she began to go to fittings for her wedding dress, I had more trouble than ever paying attention to what she was saying because I was pretty sure she really didn't know what she was doing.

"Your relationship with Herbert is moving very quickly," I said, in one attempt at intervening.

"Well," she looked up in surprise, "he loves me, and I can't wait forever."

Every time I sat across from her, I tried to make our session what we in clinical training sometimes referred to as *a safe garden*, but the truth is, I wanted to ask Rosalie if, in her entire life, she had ever screamed or wanted to scream. Maybe, I mused, I ought to be more direct and tell her something closer to what I was actually thinking, but my supervisors cautioned me to wait.

Although I had grown fond of Rosalie, I knew I'd failed in being able to lead her more quickly toward dealing with her shadowy uncle.She said she was only three when "that awful man made me feel bad."

In attempting to understand Rosalie's emotional block, I dug into my own early childhood. Before my year at the convent at age four, I had little sense of owning a body or, for that matter, a self that could act or be acted upon. At age thirty, Rosalie seemed only loosely acquainted with her true self. She had met a stranger in a public place. They had gone on some dates. Within a few months, she was talking of marriage. One day I asked Rosalie if she would like to bring Herbert in to meet me. As far as I knew, she hadn't introduced him to anyone. She asked, and he refused, perhaps wisely.

During our sessions, whenever the silence between us lasted for more than a minute, I became anxious. I could see that she was moving too fast. And—may all my supervisors forgive me— like a mother, I was hoping and praying that Herbert, who was becoming less attractive to me as the weeks went on, would become less attractive to Rosalie before it was too late.

One day Rosalie brought a photo from a fitting of her made-to-order wedding dress. The image of this beautiful snowball of a bride made me want to cry. It was useless trying to avoid judging Rosalie's choices, whether it was her potential husband or her timing, but, like a good counselor, I kept my mouth shut. I listened with what I hoped was a kind expression on my face and watched her stroke the back of one hand with the other. It occurred to me that she may have wanted to wring her hands but she chose a soothing gesture instead. It seemed as if she was petting herself, hand on hand, to calm her inexpressible emotions.

I held the bride-to-be's photo while thinking of what to say.

"You are a very attractive woman, Rosalie," I finally uttered.

A long pause followed, during which I thought about how to continue.

"So," I took a deep breath, "it looks like you've finally found what you've always wanted." I spoke slowly, looking at her inquiringly, the way my supervisor recommended. "Going with the resistance" is what he called it.

At that moment, Rosalie broke out of her hiding place. She began to cry. "I wanted to tell you all along! This feels so wrong! I thought no one would ever want me. He, Herby, says he wants me, but I don't like the *way* he wants me. I feel like an actress in an awful movie."

"It's not too late to change your mind," I said, relieved but careful not to alter my voice or posture.

This was the start of Rosalie beginning to speak about the abuse she endured when she was very young. She made connections with the way her uncle fondled her and how wrong the touching felt with Herbert. I asked her who had left this uncle alone with a three-year-old girl.

Her mother liked to get out of the house in the afternoons, Rosalie explained. She would take Rosalie's older sister, Caroline, to Girl Scouts, or visit friends before making supper.

Her mother's brother, Gustavo, lived next door, so it was convenient to ask him to watch Rosalie.

"How you must have dreaded those afternoons," I said.

She nodded, wiping her eyes. "Yes, every day."

She blew her nose softly on a perfect square of white linen that she took from her pale yellow leather handbag.

"He did odd jobs," she continued, "mowing lawns and fixing things, but he was always home late in the afternoon. Even on weekends, he'd be hanging around our yard or looking out his windows at me. I could never get away. Never."

Thankfully, at her request, Herbert speedily agreed to end their relationship. She took the wedding dress to the thrift store. "Someone might want to have it altered," she said.

Rosalie didn't answer any more ads in the personals. She admitted to hoping that someday she would find a true companion. I agreed that, yes, she ought to hope for that. In the meantime, I'm embarrassed to say, I gave her the same suggestions offered by syndicated advice columnists everywhere: that she go where she might meet other adults with similar interests, and that she get to know other single people at work.

Rosalie listened to my advice, her eyes widening at what, to her, must have seemed like unimaginable prospects. Leaning back in her chair, she allowed her body to settle into a more relaxed position. She touched her hair and her cheek, as though evaluating the possibilities of a more comfortable kind of intimacy. Before speaking again, she looked in dismay at her dainty feet, so out of proportion to her wide calves, and at her forearms, which made a definite crease at her wrists.

"I do like work," she said, finally. "I really don't know anything else."

During the middle of our third year of weekly sessions, I was preparing to retire. Rosalie continued to work on healing from her early trauma. One day, while leaving my office, she tripped on the carpet in a pair of her silky pastel pumps and a script of sorts popped into my mind. *"Say it, Rosalie,"* the mental script began. *"Shout it out: 'Someday I'm going to buy a pair of comfortable shoes.'"* But neither of us said anything. I wriggled my toes in my Birkenstocks, watching her face as she grabbed the corner of my desk to regain her balance.

I always thought it curious that Rosalie rarely displayed any rage, humor, passion, or flamboyance. I never saw a loosely tied scarf or a blouse that opened to show her throat. She had grown more courageous while working with me, but only enough to reveal her childhood secret. Everything else about her seemed to have remained the same. In three years it seemed that she had let loose only one of the numerous constraints that held her captive.

While preparing for my June retirement, I worried about leaving just as Rosalie had begun to consider living life on the other side of her abuse. During one of our last sessions, I asked her the where-do-you-see-yourself-in-five-years question.

"Maybe I'll get a promotion," she said.

I referred Rosalie to another counselor on staff, but she

didn't follow up. My inner lament about how little progress she had made during our time together lingered long after I closed her chart and filed it away for the last time. I blamed myself.

Nearly five years later, on a sunny autumn afternoon, I drove to the local apple orchard to buy some fresh cider. Walking from the parking area toward the lean-to stand, I watched a pretty, energetic woman put her two bags of apples on the ground and begin running in my direction. Her short dark hair lifted with the wind. She looked familiar. Smiling broadly, she opened her arms for a hug.

For the life of me, I didn't recognize her. I hugged her, embarrassed to have forgotten someone whom, apparently, I had known quite well.

"I'm Rosalie!" she said, laughing. "Remember me?" Her eyes were merry and her body, strong—rounded at the edges but muscular and alive. Her turtleneck, khakis, and old tweed jacket were not so different from what I was wearing.

"I've wanted to thank you for the longest time," she said. "You helped me so much!"

"I'm afraid I don't know how I helped, you," I said cautiously, "but you look wonderful."

"Well," she frowned, "you never tried to push me or change me. And you helped me figure out the hardest thing of all."

"The hardest thing?" I asked.

"You knew I was gay, right?" This was an awkward moment for both of us. As I looked down at her scuffed hiking boots, the former Rosalie's pastel shoes flashed into memory.

"I had no idea," I said.

"Well, now that you know, what do you think?" she asked. Now we were both looking down at her boots.

"I think," I said, "I would like to give you my blessing."

"Thank you," she said, looking up at me shyly and then went on. "You know, I'm happier than I've ever been. My partner and I met at a church downtown where they have a guitar Mass. Our farm is right over there, on that mountain," she pointed over my shoulder. I turned around to look at the mountain—a dark mound of evergreens interrupted by red and yellow maples. "She has an import business and works from home," Rosalie said, "and we raise sheep." She laughed at the incongruity. "They're all big and wooly now, getting ready to be shorn before it gets too cold."

We stood there for a moment, smiling shyly into each other's eyes, and then we said good-bye. Rosalie turned around to pick up her bags of apples. I walked toward the shed to buy my gallon of cider. I haven't seen her since; but every fall when I go to the orchard, I remember to look back at Rosalie's mountain, hoping it still holds the farm with the wooly sheep almost ready to be shorn and the woman she dared to love who loved her back.

# Creatures of the Deep

When my father was dying, the dolphins came. Dad called from Florida, where he and my stepmother spent their winters, to tell me not to fly down to see him, but Bob and I decided to fly south anyway. I wanted a visit before they drove back to New Jersey, afraid it might be our last.

As Bob and I checked into our hotel, my cell phone beeped with a message from my stepmother. When we reached our room, I put the phone on speaker. We listened together.

"I began driving him back this morning," she said. "Tomorrow he'll be getting his next blood transfusion in Richmond. Your father needs to be in the New Jersey hospital where the doctors know him." She didn't realize we were already in Florida.

Talking with my sister and uncle by phone that evening brought little information and no relief. My stepmother had kept my father's diagnosis secret. After calling airlines for a couple of hours in an effort to get an earlier flight back north, I sat on the bed and cried.

That night, while lying awake in the dark, I imagined my father's eyes, blue as sea glass, smiling with intelligence and pleasure as though the whole world amused him. The last time I saw him, he was standing on his porch after our annual Christmas Eve lunch, waving good-bye. Since his bypass surgery, these winter partings had the spirit of a gamble as to whether his heart would last until his scheduled return in the spring.

Having tossed the pile of bed pillows about in my sleep, I woke up more tired than I'd been the night before. My body ached. I wanted to swim. Moving through the gulf's warm waters might quiet my fears. Bob and I ate breakfast in the nearby coffee shop before driving to the ocean. I drove the rented car, windows opened wide, over seven miles of dirt roads. The overwhelming fragrance of orange blossoms from the groves helped me breathe, but didn't take away the ache.

Fort Myers Beach is handicapped accessible. It provides large wheelchairs for transporting people who need them over the sand. Two German women made a shawl of their shirts as they tried to find the perfect posture for sunning their breasts. Frail children with no hair, some with nerve and spine diseases, scuttled like sandpipers along the edge of the water. Almost everyone faced the sea, standing or sitting, limping or running. All happy to be there, they waited for the next rippling wave.

My husband, Bob, may have been the least-happy person

to be there. He was a bodysurfer, not a swimmer. With waves less than two feet high, there was no chance of surfing. Nevertheless, he very kindly headed into the water with me, wading past clusters of adults who chatted and tread water while their children floated on vinyl toys. I couldn't muster the energy to entertain Bob in any manner.

Talking didn't help a bit, but I believed that swimming would stop me from feeling lost and weepy, and I wanted no distractions. I chose a point in the water where I'd swim back and forth, parallel to the beach. "I'm just going to do my thing," I said to Bob.

I reached sideways into my crawl stroke. My head grew lighter while resting on the salty pillow. My body listed, and then stretched like an eel. As I got into the rhythm of my overhand, a silent call went out from somewhere inside me—a call of longing. The tight cords of grief eased a little.

Two dorsal fins appeared in the distance. Trusting they belonged to dolphins, I kept my pace, checking the beach on my right and then looking over my left shoulder, tracking the sleek mammals until they disappeared underwater. Feeling a displacement on my left and drawn into its sudden vacuum, I sprang away to avoid an accidental encounter. The dolphin raised its head. For an instant, we were side by side, eye to eye. I did some quiet sidestrokes. This seemed to bring us to a kind of mutual understanding. Relieved, I eased back into my overhand, thinking peaceful thoughts toward this creature.

I'd feared my initial jerking away might have scared the

dolphin off, but he stayed. He *stayed*. My pronouns may be wrong—the dolphin could have been a he or a she. I knew only that this creature treated me like a good parent or true friend. I began to feel an immense mysterious trust as we swam about a half mile together, back and forth, back and forth. For a while, he kept to the path I had chosen. Changing strokes gave me intervals of rest. I would start with the crawl, and then the sidestroke, backstroke, and breaststroke. The dolphin followed me like the mirror of my best hour.

The dolphin then breached the surface, and his entire form became visible. Cutting cleanly through the water, as though confident of our developing bond, he swam ahead, rocking me a little in his wake. I let him channel me through the warm water. I became relaxed, even drowsy. Our eyes met once more in a sideways glance before he swam away.

Standing, a little shaky, I watched the dolphin's slow retreat. Bob stood in waist-high water about fifty feet away from me. Another dolphin swam from his line of vision toward the horizon. Two dolphins' fins drew silver streaks across the surface.

He described the second dolphin's approach, how it swam around him in circles until Bob became free enough to join in the play. My amazement doubled as I wondered how a wild creature could know how to involve my shy husband in extended frolic. The rest of the day I tried to defend myself against expecting that my friendship with this water creature could continue.

The next morning, I woke beneath my collection of hotel pillows with more disturbing concerns. My uncle told me that my dad, now in the New Jersey hospital, was hanging on by a thread and that I should prepare myself to lose him.

After breakfast, at my urging, Bob went with me, again, to the beach. My hunger for the sea was stronger than ever. Some people hunger for liquor and count the hours until their first drink of the day. Even after eliminating wheat products from my diet, I used to salivate just thinking about a torn-off piece of hot semolina bread dipped in a dish of olive oil spotted with slices of garlic and cayenne flakes. For me, getting into a warm ocean represents a more passionate hunger. The very smell of the sea comes over me like the ether of roses.

Bob put a canvas chair in the shadow of the pier and waded into the water. After swimming a few strokes underwater, he got out and headed straight for his book of crossword puzzles.

I looked out over an ocean devoid of silver streaks. I slid into my crawl. Swimming companionless in this wide sandy basin would have to be enough. With every reach, I tried to practice expecting nothing, yet my whole being called out for yesterday's friend.

And then, rolling into the vacuum and feeling a sudden rush of water against my left side, I knew that the dolphin, *my* dolphin, had come. Lifted by the surge, I almost swooned. We swam together on that second day, more evenly, as equals. Thinking he'd sensed my hurt made it easier to believe I would see my dad again. Dying isn't always fast. My father, I assured myself, would live until I got back.

I slept well that night. During my next early morning call, my uncle said that my dad was holding on. In just two days, I'd grown stronger, with new muscles forming in my upper arms. Half-mile swims had never been part of my daily workout. The dolphin's presence seemed to be strengthening my soul as well as my body. His nearness, his steadiness, encouraged me to reach into the deeper waters of my life. My earthly father, who also loved the sea, seemed as close to me as he'd ever been.

My dad had been swimming out of range since I was a toddler. Recently, my cousin found the last existing photo of my parents and me among her father's effects. We were at the beach. My father held me while my beautiful mother sat near us on the sand. They would eventually separate while I was in the convent school. Later, when we lived in my grandparents' row house, my dad's visits became sporadic. After my mother's remarriage, he adhered to her legal request for no contact until we reached eighteen, the age of emancipation.

When my father and I met again, I was nineteen and a student at Columbia University. He didn't want to hear what I had waited so long to tell him—that I'd missed him so much and missed him still. Caught in the undertow of an emotional riptide, I hid my sinking, my drowning, in a maze of confusion and poor choices. I wanted to be his child again.

Early on the morning of our flight back to New York, Fort Myers Beach was filled mostly with joggers and old men with their dogs. When my dolphin came to swim with me, I thanked him. Not with words, but with the same inner call that went out before our first meeting. He taught me how feeling, deep feeling—the language we both understood— carries over distance. I knew him immediately when the water was displaced by his approaching. Our communication may have been more meaningful because it was mostly hidden, under the surface of our souls. The dolphin never touched me—not a brushing of a fin on my arm, no gentle nudge—and I never reached out to stroke his face, although he came close enough.

On the short flight home, Bob and I didn't talk much. He did the Sunday crossword puzzle while I thought about the ancient lore in which dolphins represent the Christ. Whittlers have carved the dolphin's image into the figureheads of hand-hewn boats. Sometimes the dolphin's form would be mounted on a little cross to in memory of shipwrecked sailors or anyone who fell into the sea. I didn't need to be carried to shore, only to be shored up.

Against the drone of the plane's engines, I fell into a meditation on the creatures we keep as pets and those we kill for food. We humans, in believing that we're superior to other creatures, are missing out on forms of intelligence and compassion that might be greater than our own. Studying mutual respect and mutual gentleness between different species might bring us to a better understanding of ourselves and others.

The next day at the hospital I entered my father's room and found my stepmother sitting in a chair next to his bed. She never left his side. She had always seemed to be guarding him against everything and everyone, especially me. My father's face conveyed a struggle. He didn't open his eyes, but he knew I was there. He squeezed my hand and tried to sit up, pushing toward consciousness. I wanted to look into his eyes even if he could not look into mine. His eyes had the translucency of glass filed down by a thousand years of sea sand to the element of blue. When I put my hand on his forehead, he stopped struggling and relaxed.

My stepmother got up and left the room. *Thank you, thank you,* I thought. Standing outside the open door with a group of relatives, she declared in a loud whisper, "She's praying!"

My stepmother's announcement annoyed me. The truth is, at that moment, I had no prayer that she or anyone there would recognize. Looking toward the door, I silently invited Jesus into the room to be with my father and me. That was all I could manage. After a while, I felt the call go out from my inner ocean, like the call that first led the dolphin to my side. Remembering my friend in the saltiness of my tears became both prayer and solace.

In the next few days, I needed to return to my work at the counseling agency. News of my father's death brought no surprise. I learned later on that, during his last hour, the client in my office at the time had been telling me how her parents never truly accepted her. A successful educator in her own right, she still felt that they set higher standards for her than she could ever achieve.

Although I had tried for a number of years to solicit my father's love and acceptance, I remain thankful for our slowly developing relationship. When I was in my fifties and he in his seventies, and could still drive, he would meet for breakfast halfway between his house and my church. The diner we frequented, with its shiny steel exterior, reminded me of a big white whale. There, in conversation, we became easy with one another. He learned to go deeper. Taught to hide his feelings as a boy, he was able to speak to me about his pain at the death of a close friend. While he'd sometimes playfully call me Apple Blossom, like he did when I was very small, more often he'd engage me as family priest and trusted confidant.

Surely, God stepped in again to heal the pain of my loss. For weeks after my father died, I would dream of my dolphin moving through the water to meet me, coming through the door of its own wild heart to swim beside me.

# Roses from Lisieux

Saints befriended me long before I befriended other children. The summer of my ninth year, Saint Francis surprised me in the backyard of my maternal grandparents' shore bungalow. Boom-Pa, my grandfather, had attached a screened aviary to the side of their garage so their pet canaries and parakeets could enjoy the warmer weather. One morning, the birds began to sing all at once alerting me to Francis' presence. I looked up from where I sat on the sandstone driveway and there he was, standing on the far side of the garage, in colors of light, a little above the ground.

While living within my new family constellation in northwest New Jersey, a variety of heaven-sent friends colored my meditations, even after I joined the neighborhood children's adventures. Now, when reminded, I celebrate the memory of the saints on their feast days. Most mainline Protestants tend to regard honoring the canonized as interfering with one's direct relationship with God. For me the saints provided, and still provide welcome company and help along the way.

Many years passed between my visit from Saint Francis and the time I came upon what seemed to me a material sign of Saint Thérèse of Lisieux, also referred to as The Little Flower.

Even though I lived hours away, I was asked to officiate at both funeral and graveside services of one of my former parishioners, Amanda, as her current pastor was too ill to preside. The torrential rain pouring onto the path leading from Amanda's gravesite to the parked cars provided a backdrop for our grief. As I left the protection of the tarp awning, words from the liturgy still sang in my mind: ". . . yet even at the grave we make our song: Alleluia, alleluia, alleluia."⁹—incredible sadness pierced by incredible hope.

I walked carefully with the others along the muddy road while the wet wind whipped at my face. When I looked down, I saw a fresh, peach-hued rose land on top of my sandal. "A rose from Amanda," I said under my breath. Bending to pick it up, I felt a rush of warmth. Its pale color didn't match other roses around the gravesite, and I was mystified by its being almost dry in spite of the wind and rain. Ordinary wind has no property of intention, but I believe the Holy Spirit has. When

---

⁹ Twelve words from the Commendation from <u>The Book of Common Prayer</u> (1662). "Extracts from the Book of Common Prayer, the rights of which are vested in the Crown, are reproduced by permission of the Crown's Patentee, Cambridge University Press."

I got to my car I put the rose in a water bottle and brushed its petals lightly with my fingers.

Amanda's family had chosen a lakeside restaurant for hosting the memorial lunch. There were flowers and candles on every table. We could choose from a selection of continental dishes and wines. Surrounded by his loving clan, Joe, Amanda's husband, began to relax. In a gesture I remembered from happier occasions, he transferred a piece of ravioli from his plate to mine.

"*You* can eat!" he used to say to me with a mix of admiration and admonishment. He said it that day, too, laughing as though he'd forgotten the reason for this luncheon.

Just as Amanda's suffering had ended, Joe's was about to begin. I had glimpsed the start of his diminishment the night before. From the back of the empty funeral parlor, Joe's son, Matt, and I watched Joe approach Amanda's open casket. His tentative stance, the rounding of his shoulders, sketched an image different from the man we knew.

"He will never be the same," we said to each other.

Soon Joe would have the solitude he always said he wanted but never actually embraced. When I was the couple's pastor, Joe spent a lot of time in his basement workshop. Amanda confided that, in his later years, he had all but stopped reaching out to her with affection. He'd squander his delight on a couple of baby raccoons he would invite to creep from the deck of their home onto their dining room carpet. The critters would come inside for the almonds and dried fruit Joe would leave out for them. When it wasn't raccoon season, Joe would stroke and speak tenderly to his cat, Susie, who liked to lie on one of their home's sunny windowsills. Although Joe seemed to hold back his tenderness from the humans he loved most, I saw his aloofness as disguise rather than substance.

Some time before Amanda's death, Joe and I spent an entire day waiting in a New York hospital while Amanda had heart surgery. He picked me up at six o'clock in the morning, and we drove in silence through dark-to-dawn traffic. During the nine-hour procedure, Joe made sure that one or the other of us was always in the waiting room. I'd go to the cafeteria to get us fruit, yogurt, and sandwiches, which we'd eat slowly. Stretching out our refreshments helped the hours go by. At other times we paced, leafed through magazines, and sat for long periods with our eyes closed in thought, prayer, or worry. When the doctor finally led us to the recovery room, Amanda lay seemingly plasticized under a bundle of tubes and wires. Joe's gasp was louder than the sound of her mechanical breathing. It seemed that his wanting me there was actually his wanting God to be there, albeit in the form of my imperfect representation. I believe his practiced veneer of indifference hid an utterly devoted heart.

Midway through Amanda's memorial feast, I left Joe's table to sit at the other tables, visiting briefly with each guest. I enjoyed a rare and lasting reciprocity with this family. Even after my appointment to a counseling agency out of the area, they continued to care for me, and I for them. Amanda and I had kept in touch. We'd always say "I love you" at the end of our phone conversations and I would often stop by to visit with her and Joe on my trips to New Jersey.

When at last I walked over to say good-bye to Joe, I felt compelled to mention the rose.

"Something happened at the gravesite," I began.

"I know," he said matter-of-factly. "I saw the rose fall out of the sky."

Having a witness to the occurrence pulled me back into the scene. "It landed right on my sandal," I said. "Where could it have come from?"

"You're the minister," he said. "You tell me."

As Joe grew cautious, I did too. Joe used to close his eyes during my sermons, so I knew I was taking a chance here.

"The rose seemed like a spark of Amanda's spirit," I said. "A loving gesture. I'm sure that Matt would like to hear about it."

"So tell him," he said.

"It would mean more if you told him," I replied, even though I knew he never would. Joe's emotional caution blocked any tenderness, even toward his son and even on this day.

When I arrived for work at the counseling agency on Monday morning, I went directly to my colleague Justine's office. I'd recognized how her Catholic faith gave spiritual depth to her clinical practice, so I told her about the rose landing on top of my sandal in the rain.

"You were sad about losing your friend," she said thoughtfully.

After I confessed to weeping while conducting the funeral service at the church, Justine turned around to take a small volume from her bookshelf.

"Look up Saint Thérèse of Lisieux," she said. "Therese is known for sending down roses to people in grief."

During breaks throughout that day, I read about Thérèse, who became a nun at fifteen and joined a cloistered convent in Lisieux, France. During her short life she served in her community by doing menial tasks. She was known for always being compassionate and cheerful toward everyone, but I wondered if she ever felt profound sadness. Later in my own spiritual journey, I learned about her development as a writer and spiritual leader and how it took thousands of years for the church to see in her an inspired bearer of God's love. One of her two biological sisters who were also nuns in the Lisieux convent compiled and published her autobiography, *The Story of a Soul,* after Thérèse's death at age twenty-four from tuberculosis. She had declared how she wanted to spend her eternity—by sending down roses from heaven as a sign of enduring hope.

I pressed the lovely pale rose inside an antique Bible I owned, but somehow it disappeared. It may have fallen out from underneath the heavy, copper-tooled cover during a move.

---

After my formal retirement from full-time ministry, Bob and I rented an apartment in Lauderdale-by-the-Sea, a quiet strip of land with bougainvilleas growing in the door yards. Since serving as parish pastor, I'd dreamed of writing a book on preaching without notes. Although I did a meager amount of household chores in our small apartment, I wanted to imitate St. Thérèse as a spiritual teacher. I longed to be able to inspire the mostly male ecclesiastical establishment to respect and improve their preaching. For two hours every morning and two hours every afternoon I'd sit at the table in our apartment's living room, keying in new chapters and revising old ones.

Every sunny day around four o'clock, I'd float on my back in our pool, searching the sky for a sign that my efforts would succeed. Following the floating meditations, I'd walk to the beach, sometimes with Bob, sometimes alone. Bob and I agreed to acknowledge our good fortune of finding a place just a few blocks from the sea by going there at least once a day. We called it "going to look at the ocean." "Going to look at the ocean" nearly always gave me a lift. After supper, I'd edit the day's printout.

For the first couple of months of working on my book, gratitude alone kept me on track. I was grateful to be where there was no winter. I was grateful for having what seemed to be a worthwhile project and a supportive husband, but not everything was smooth sailing. Part of my research required me to visit a variety of south Florida churches. After attending a service, I'd talk with the preacher for a few minutes. Most admitted they'd never tried to separate themselves from their sermon script, while others were understandably proud of relying exclusively on notes. Even younger pastors and priests, fresh from seminary, would stand in their pulpits, their eyes focused on their manuscripts, and hardly ever glance toward their people. A few would look out at their parishioners, now and then, but they'd go back to reading so quickly, we had to strain to catch every word.

The statistics, lost forever, required reconstituting my research results. Of the approximately thirty random interdenominational pastors I spoke with, only two spoke from a manuscript with an air of grace. Six were proud to have preached from one page of notes, and only three stood before their congregations, homework done and paperless, trusting to receive the Spirit's guidance without props.

Years of listening to audio tapes drew me to this book project, and watching videos of my own and others' preaching brought both pain and pleasure. In one of my earliest attempts before the camera, my message came from Paul's Letter to the Hebrews and centered on being "surrounded by so great a cloud of witnesses."[10] When I watched the recording of that sermon immediately after the taping, I noticed with interest my sometimes clumsy attempts to order my thoughts without benefit of any written guide. Although I cringed at these reminders of my anxiety, I was never bored. Instead, I discovered that brief silences and occasional glances toward the ceiling could create an assurance that the preacher wasn't simply running from

---

[10] Heb 12:1, NRSV

word to word but was trying to listen for God's voice (which, in fact, I was). While tangling with the mystery of invisible saints becoming visible, I forgot about making a perfect delivery and abandoned myself to the cadence of natural speech. I've been testing this style on congregations ever since.

As the winter solstice shortened the number of hours of available sunlight, my days in Florida started to wear on me. I dreaded the prospect of spending Christmas so far from home, and I was discouraged by the number of seemingly disengaged pastors I'd encountered. Very few of them considered practicing sermon delivery a lifelong commitment. I had to push myself to continue writing. The rose that fell out of the sky a few years back had been forgotten. In spite of all the good in my life, I felt unsupported in my new work and goals.

By January, I had succumbed to the shifting sands. My perspectives on marriage and retirement came into question. My digestive issues worsened. Perhaps I had taken a wrong turn. Maybe I should have worked at the counseling agency for another year. Saint Paul may have been right about people in ministry staying single if they were single when called, and married if they were married when called. My personal history reveals lower scores as wife and mother than as pastor and counselor.

Attempts to adjust my focus failed. Continuing to write with no identifiable readership or publication strategy brought me to a hopeless junction. Intending to provide comfort, Bob reminded me that in a few weeks we would return home to our familiar life. I stuck to my writing schedule, sans enthusiasm. I tried to find whatever peace I could by swimming in the ocean and savoring the taste of my homemade Mexican pie, but no earthly pleasure can move a soul in stasis, and none of my remedies could save my manuscript through this crisis of self-doubt.

On the Ides of March, right after supper, I collected my notes, printouts, and backup disks and rolled them up in an old, giant-sized T-shirt. I tied them with cord I'd been using to wrap items for the car trip home. Bob, watching the evening news, didn't see me walk past him with my burden. I think he would have stopped me if he had. Lost love was hidden in the heavy bundle I carried close to my heart. My desire to write something to glorify God had failed. I couldn't forget my many concerns long enough to write as freely as Saint Thérèse had written or as freely as I hoped to teach other pastors to preach. Ashamed, I imagined young Thérèse's words pouring forth with no interfering pride, no worries about their success or longevity. Thoroughly discouraged, I decided to discard my Pharisee self in one final, irrevocable act.

I went out into a darkness speckled with tiny Christmas lights some misguided resort managers weave around palm tree barks without realizing how they bind and hurt the trees. When I reached a nearby green metal dumpster, I opened the lid and threw six months' worth of work into its cavernous belly. The paper and disks made a dull thud as they landed on top of flattened milk cartons and old newspapers. When I let go of the lid, it slammed down with the sound of a gunshot. I went back to my rented rooms, half in misery, half in relief, to use Bob as a crying pillow. A part of me hoped he would go outside and retrieve it, but instead he put his arms around me and said, "This is what I'm here for." At first I wanted to punch him, but, on reflection I have to admit that this man always gave me plenty of soul space.

On one of our last days before we drove home, we were walking barefoot along the beach in the late afternoon. Every few minutes we would stop to look out across the ocean, pausing to admire the beauty of the water in the changing light. Bob was his usual appreciative, self-contained being, while my furtive heart lumbered on. I was searching for something to reassure me that, although I had wasted my self-appointed sabbatical, I might still be called to create something of value in this life.

We had reached a shelf of rock where the water eddies when I saw an object under the water near my feet. The sea's churning revealed a flash of red, round like a ball, being pulled this way and that.

"What?" I exclaimed, twisting my body around to follow it. Bob, nearby, looked down as I reached into the water to close my hand around the feathery lightness. Standing up, I shouted over the sound of crashing waves, "A rose from Saint Thérèse!"

"It came right into your hand," Bob said, shaking his head. Once again, I had a witness, someone whose place in the world could be trusted.

I examined the petals. Except for some slight bruising from the salt water, there was no blemish, no brokenness. Throughout the evening I kept an eye on the rose, which I'd put in a bowl of water on the kitchen windowsill. My cheeks began to ache from smiling. Perhaps it wasn't too late. Perhaps something new could be born in me despite the presumed ignominy of retirement.

By morning, when the rose was beginning to close in on itself, I knew that I wouldn't be blamed for what I couldn't accomplish in a season. I promised the God in me that, however long it took, I would learn patience. The clear vision—the joy—of the child within me would be restored.

I remember one day, long ago, when I was preaching in an empty classroom in front of a video camera, how I pictured the saints standing along the walls as still as blue herons against the camouflage of heaven. My vision became real when, a few years later while visiting a newly built Greek Orthodox Church in south Florida, I saw a modern artist's life-sized paintings of their saints, one on each panel of the church's inner sanctuary. My favorite was Saint Helen, who wore small single-drop earrings.

Truly, the saints are all around us whether they make themselves known by visions, or by tokens from the sky or from the sea. Most of the time, they offer no tokens at all and remain unseen. Yet even when we become discouraged at failing to discern their manner of appearing, they illuminate our paths beyond our sight.

# Love Story

Nigel had called my spiritual director to ask if he knew of someone in the area who might be willing to visit his brother, Hank. Hank wasn't a member of the church where I served as visitation minister, or of any church, but his health was in decline. Nigel thought it might help to have a pastor listen to his brother's fears. I agreed to meet with him in his home and wound up doing so with some regularity.

Hank's apartment was dark. A gray cloud of cigarette smoke hung near the entrance of the hallway. The windows of its main room faced northwest and seemed to always be in the shade. The smoke made me cough and clung to my hair and clothes. A glass ashtray overflowing with cigarillo butts rested on the middle cushion of the couch. Hank sat on one side of it and I sat on the other side. After a brief greeting, his wife, Cindy, kept busy with dishes and other tasks in their single-walled kitchenette.

Hank's thinking was sometimes jumbled. His wife

appeared to have similar challenges. Hank confessed to his sin of smoking while lighting up another cigarillo. Cindy had emphysema and also smoked. I quickly learned that for many folks with disabling conditions, nicotine is the drug of choice. Because of the air quality in their apartment, I wore a personal ionizer on my future visits. Attached to a cord and worn like a necklace, the ionizer removes about eighty-five percent of smoke and other irritants around one's face. A floppy wool beret kept the smoky residue from my hair.

"I know they're evil," Hank once said, holding up a nearly empty pack of cigarillos. His voice sounded as if it were being pulled up slowly from some deep and difficult place inside his chest. "I try to stop, but the devil tempts me." He wagged his head from side to side. "I just can't seem to stop."

Hank coughed hard to clear his windpipe. Recovering, he smiled sheepishly and then called out, "Cindy, are you going to the store?"

"Yes. I'm going to the store," Cindy answered with her little half smile. "Do you need anything, Honey?" As she approached, I heard her wheeze.

"Honey," he repeated in a gravelly voice. "She calls me Honey because she loves me." Teary joy lit up his eyes.

"Come on," Cindy insisted, her smile widening at the endearment. "Tell me what you want. I'll go so you two can have your privacy."

Cindy always seemed uncomfortable around me, and I thought she may have had trouble with the idea of a female clergy person. At first I tried to ease her concerns and did everything I could to include her in our activities. When that didn't work, I did everything I could to kindly exclude her.

"Hank and I are going to pray now," I'd say. "You can just keep doing what you're doing."

For several months Cindy would go to the store on the days when I visited. A few minutes after my arrival, she'd pace back and forth. Before leaving for the store, a Spanish bodega on the corner, she'd limp over to Hank, brushing past me, and put her arms around him. He would reach up and put his arms around her.

"Goodbye, love," he'd groan in his odd basso.

"Bye, Honey," she'd say, kissing him on the mouth. "This is the part I like!"

I think she meant the kissing. Since both she and Hank had lost some teeth, the sight of their intimacy shook me at first. Yet something else, something subtle and irresistible, drew me in. I admit that I felt more than a touch of envy at their show of affection. With physical and developmental disabilities so profound that they needed a caseworker to arrange the practical details of their lives, their overt fondness for each other surprised me. They seemed incapable of guile.

While Cindy walked to and from the bodega, Hank and I bowed our heads. Hank was always in the mood for prayer. He wanted reassurance that his sins wouldn't damn him forever. Taking the cue from him and a tip from his brother, Nigel, I rationalized his smoking habit to ease his mind.

"There are some people who just have to smoke." I told him. "It's like taking medicine to help you relax."

Hank then confessed to committing sins worse than smoking. This very frail and old-looking man of only fifty years was referring to the sins of his youth but didn't name even one of them.

Returning from the store, Cindy arrived breathless, carrying a liter of cola and a pack of cigarillos. Hank and I had finished our prayer. Our talk, though halting, went on for another half hour while Cindy busied herself around the apartment. A kind of poetry found its way into Hank's speech. His sentences often had the stark brevity of the phrases children invent while day dreaming or singing when they think no one else can hear them. He told me about his dialysis treatments, expressing both his reluctance and submission in a few words. "I don't want to do it," he said. When Hank spoke, his words weren't separated; they were always attached to the next word by a connecting tone. "But I've got to do it to stay alive," he added.

"He's got to do it to stay alive," Cindy echoed, as though I hadn't understood. She may have been right. I could think of no appropriate response to his lament, so I simply nodded in agreement and curbed my impulse to offer helpful information.

"I have to do it to stay alive," Hank said once more, as though that was all that needed saying.

In the silence that followed, Hank placed his cigarillo into a groove in the ashtray and studied his hands. Cindy went to the sink, filled a glass with water, and swallowed a pill. After a while I turned to Hank.

"So, what are you thinking about?" I asked.

"Death," he said. "I'm thinking about my death."

He knew where kidney failure led, but whether or not Cindy knew was unclear. Holes existed in her view of reality, while Hank's view, although clearer, was marked with oblique meanings, at times impossible to interpret.

I watched while Cindy took another pill and gulped it down. Her hand shook. Whether it was a tremor or a reaction to Hank's reference to his death, I didn't know. She continued to move about the room with dogged purpose, setting the table and taking containers out of the refrigerator for supper. Hank and I sat on the couch on either side of the glass ashtray of cigarillo butts without speaking until I got up to hug each of them and say good-bye.

Some months into our visits, when Cindy had given Hank his good-bye kiss, she put her hands on my shoulders for balance and leaned over to kiss my forehead. Her long, graying hair brushed against my cheek. I have to admit that, in spite of our initial mutual discomfort, we belonged to each other in some strange way. I always hugged Hank and Cindy, yet I never progressed to returning Cindy's kisses. Their tenderness wounded me. I'd never seen anything like it, and, worse, had never enjoyed such easy affection in my marital alliances. Often I wondered how these two people were able to get along so well in that dark apartment with the worn-out furniture and the scratched pots and pans. I couldn't understand how they were able to continue their courting and banter given the painfully evident struggles of their daily lives. The haze of smoke they created may have offered some cover for them, but for me it brought a stinging revelation of my earlier selves. Being kissed by Cindy over months of greetings and partings had taken me to a humbler, shakier place.

Whatever life with my husband lacked, it wasn't clean air, shiny pots and pans, or an attractive home. After selling our real estate, we were modestly comfortable. We spent the winter months at a Florida resort. Yet we were severely handicapped in one important way: We hadn't yet grown into the ease of loving. We both had ego issues, pride, secrets, and interfering personal investments. I worried about a number of things, such as my health and appearance and trying to find a way to retire without sinking into oblivion. Bob clung to the safety of his New England reserve. Sometimes it seemed as though his reticence was more dangerous than cigarillo smoke, sucking all the oxygen out of the air.

The difference between Bob's and my style of engaging and Hank's and Cindy's style was striking. Bob and I played house, and we played couple by wearing matching outfits during the first years of our marriage. Being relaxed together wasn't easy, especially on weekends. Bob was completely retired, a big reader, and a somewhat obsessive thinker. Sunday's crossword puzzle remained on our dining room table, untouchable in the process, until Tuesday or Wednesday. His worst fault, in my opinion, was his addiction to televised sports while mine was restlessness. I had grown weary of part-time work involvements, and our marriage was beginning to seem like one of them. Sometimes Bob would drive me to Hank's on snowy winter afternoons and pick me up an hour later. The juxtaposition of my time with him and my time with Hank and Cindy seemed to highlight what my husband and I lacked.

While Bob and I existed in our well-concealed strife, every day Hank and Cindy began a new feast of love. Once, after arriving half an hour late for my visit, I found that Cindy had already prepared their evening meal: canned vegetables with chicken cooked in a ruined Teflon pot and tall glasses of Hawaiian Punch with ice.

"Go ahead and eat," I said as I sat on the couch at a respectful distance. They were unselfconscious in my presence. Watching them, I saw the mundane become exquisite as they met each other's every requirement, from casual endearments to infinite smokes.

One afternoon Cindy stayed in the bedroom instead of going to the store. She listened through the half-opened door to Hank's and my prayer time. I always slowed the Lord's Prayer[11] way down for Hank and quieted my voice so that his drawn-out speech would dominate. I hoped that hearing his own voice speaking the word *forgive* might soften his image of God. Looking up, I saw Cindy limping out to where we sat, tears streaming down her face.

"That is so beautiful!" she cried. "Say it again."

---

[11] Mt 6:1–13

She sat down and blew her nose into a handful of tissues. Hank and I said it again, after which Cindy composed herself and sat staring at the tablecloth that held the Communion wafers and grape juice. In the silence that followed, I noticed that the flower pattern on their old plastic tablecloth had lost most of its color. Its flowers had been worn right down to its gray flannel base. The next time I visited, they had a bright new tablecloth. I remarked on it.

"Our caseworker brought it," Cindy said. "We love Penny!"

Penny and I met once when our visits coincided. Right away, we saw each other as persons separate from our official helping roles. We each had become Hank's and Cindy's friend. Neither of them had family nearby to look in on them. Hank had a brother, Fred, in the same town, but Fred wasn't in a position to assume supervision of their care. It was Hank's brother Nigel who brought us all together. Nigel and his wife, Louisa, both professionals, visited faithfully during the summer and over the winter holidays, and they checked in regularly with Hank and Cindy by phone.

In little more than a year, changes came about in our visits. Cindy no longer took off for the bodega during prayer time. She stayed close, resting her elbows on the flowers of the plastic tablecloth, waiting to hear the Lord's Prayer.[12] I had been celebrating Communion with Hank, just the two of us, on alternate months until the moment Cindy pulled up a chair

---

[12] ibid.

to the table and solemnly reached out her hand to receive the wafer.

One day something happened that ended our monthly afternoons together. Hank fell while he was out with Cindy on their weekly shopping trip. Emergency responders transported him to a hospital. Cindy, failing to find out which hospital had admitted him, sobbed uncontrollably in her phone call to Penny. Penny comforted Cindy and took her to see for herself that Hank was all right. The fall had only dislocated his shoulder. Then she helped Cindy make preparations to take him home.

Our collective relief was short-lived, however. Hank fell again in his apartment, causing further damage to his shoulder. After a brief hospitalization, he was admitted to a local nursing home. I expected this would end their amazing closeness, but I was wrong. They kept in touch mostly by phone. Their face-to-face encounters continued, but they were difficult because of the institutional setting and Cindy's fears.

The nursing facility had to replace the bed in Hank's room with a foam rubber mattress to keep him safely near the floor. When I visited, I sat on the floor on top of my folded coat. Hank sat on his mattress bed, propped up against the wall with pillows. Each time I saw him, which was more frequently now, the bandage covering his shoulder got bigger.

We shared Communion in his room. On a day when there was no grape juice or wafers at church, I grabbed a container of apple juice and cut out circles of white bread with a knife to serve as wafers. Feeling apologetic about the substitutions, I spread a linen napkin on the edge of his mattress before placing the tiny cups of juice and the circles of bread on the gold metal tray from my Communion box. Noticing the pale juice and store-bought bread, Hank frowned. He kept looking at me as though he wanted to ask a question. Maybe, I thought, he wanted to ask if there was something wrong, if God was really there with us.

I said no formal liturgy, just offered the gift itself: "Body of Christ—the bread of heaven. Blood of Christ—the cup of salvation."

While I washed and dried the cups and tray in a room off the nurse's station, a male aide lifted Hank off his floor mattress and strapped him into a wheelchair. I wheeled him to the elevator. Along the way, a nurse handed me a cigarette lighter and gave Hank his allotted two cigarettes. We took the elevator down to the facility's receiving station, which was the only area in the building where patients could smoke. Sometimes in that dark concrete space as Hank sat in his wheelchair and I stood nearby, we seemed to be celebrating another sort of communion. The white paper cigarettes brought forth a different ritual, with different prayers and conversations.

I touched each cigarette with the flame of the lighter. Hank managed only a couple of weak inhalations before stamping them out on the basement floor. When he thanked me, his eyes watered with gratitude. He no longer regarded his smokes as sinful portents of hellfire. Between the two of us, his cigarettes became tokens of trust and friendship. It seemed certain that the devil he had once imagined pursuing him had fled from disuse.

One afternoon, after his smokes, Hank and I were about to take the elevator back to his room when he said, "You never feel bad or guilty." I misunderstood his statement to be a question.

"Sure I do," I told him. "I think nearly everyone feels bad or guilty sometimes."

"No," he moaned in some kind of torture for having to explain. "I'm not talking about *everybody*. I mean you! *You* can't feel bad or guilty."

As with many of our conversations, I could find no entry point. No response came to mind. I had to wait for him to speak again.

"You are perfect," he said finally, with a touch of longing, pulling out each word as he always did. I could only guess he meant my education or my ordination, or maybe, simply, that, unlike him, I appeared to be relatively healthy.

How close to imperfect I knew myself to be! Part-time visitation work left me with a sense of being on the fringe of more vibrant ministries. At home, my restlessness threatened to end our marriage. My family history of escaping relationships, especially those most important to our lives, went back to my maternal great-grandfather, who abandoned his wife soon after his daughter, my grandmother, turned eighteen. As a pastor and counselor, my attendance record was steadfast. As a private person, I spent years moving on, cutting ties, and burning bridges. While wheeling Hank to the elevator that afternoon to take him back to his room, it seemed as though my years of faithful service hadn't changed me at all.

Hank endured surgeries, pain, and weeks in the intensive care unit. The hospital staff recognized his patience and purity of heart. They, too, learned to listen to his words. I wish I had written down more of them, especially during his last days. His affectionate nature, not limited to his bond with Cindy, offered the same ease of loving to everyone he met.

Penny, who was curious about Hank's faith journey, visited him in the ICU.

"Tell me about your relationship with Jesus," she said.

Hank thought for a while, as he often did before speaking. "Jesus," he said, "loves the least the most."

If Hank's comfort in being "the least" was in being the most loved, he was right on. Deep regard for Hank flowed, and not only from Jesus, his family, Penny, and me. Even Hank's doctors went beyond polite formality to engage him. I overheard the ICU staff swapping stories about Hank's courage and kindness. He had a good word for everyone, and every one of those words had to be drawn up from a canyon of pain along with enough breath to produce the tone that welded them together.

I don't remember the day Hank died. I do remember holding his hand in the ICU and sitting in an outer room for a long time, waiting for Nigel and Louisa to come out. That may or may not have been the day of his leaving.

I led a memorial service in the chapel of the church where I was visitation minister. The chapel was small but airy and had maple benches with blue cushions. Blue stained-glass windows filtered the late morning sun. Folks came from social services, the nursing facility, the ICU staff; the service was filled with everyone who had helped Hank on his journey home. Nigel and Louisa, Fred, Cindy, Penny, and an old friend of Nigel's all sat in a cluster close to the chancel. We sang and prayed together.

In my meditation, I told about a visit of Nigel to his brother, Hank, in the nursing home. Nigel had wheeled Hank down to the basement so Hank could enjoy two of his daily ration of cigarettes. After his smokes, Hank began to make long, strange-sounding vocalizations held together by unintelligible words. This lasted quite a while before Nigel asked, "What are you trying to say, Hank?"

"I am singing you a song," Hank replied.

It seemed the Spirit once more had carried Hank beyond his assigned limitations.

After the service, Nigel invited everyone for lunch at a fine old restaurant. With twelve or more people, our group filled the long table, which was set with white linen, sparkling glasses of water, and baskets of bread. Seated on the side that faced a sunny window, I took the glare with grace. Partial blinding seemed just right on this day of ritual parting.

Nigel brought family photos to share with everyone. To shield the sun's brightness, I tilted my fingers over the edge of each glossy print to see the three brothers—Hank, Fred, and Nigel—waving and smiling while standing by a lake, happy by the water, happy among the trees. Nigel looked closely at each photograph and shared a brief memory before handing it to the person on his right. At one point, before moving on to the next image, he took a sip of wine and wept. Although wine and weeping seem to go together at memorial lunches, I marveled at this man of many gifts grieving so openly for his disabled brother.

I knew, sitting there, caught in that ray of sunlight, that the whole story of life, from beginning to end, has to do with the ease of loving. I first discovered it in that dark apartment on winter afternoons while being confided in by Hank and kissed by Cindy. There, my most intimate, most alien selves showed up; I saw how much they wanted to be kissed and listened to. I could no longer turn away.

Since then, I've learned how the ease of loving remains relaxed at heart, even through the hardest trials. It knows how to rejoice and how to return to rejoicing. I try, regularly, to practice this ease of loving. It's a little like practicing the resurrection—the coming up out of a tomb of darkness into the light. For me, attaining this has been difficult. The crush of earth obstructs my efforts. It requires heavenly assistance at every turn.

In my relationship with Bob, this ease of loving involves much more than romance; it offers a well of comfort and a trusting playfulness. With my son, a new closeness is forming although our communications are mostly restricted to phone calls and e-mails. My practice of the ease of loving is not limited to relationships with family and friends. In meeting strangers everywhere, I try to cherish each encounter.

It was Hank who taught me to bring up each thought, each word, from the same mysterious, unconsidered depth.

# Christ in the Lecture Hall

F right accompanied my diagnosis of scleroderma, an autoimmune connective tissue disease that is, so far, incurable. Scleroderma strikes about as many people as multiple sclerosis yet it remains lesser known. When I became a member of the Scleroderma Foundation in 2008, I joined a support group for patients. A few years later I became a facilitator for that group, began attending lectures, and wrote about living with the disease. However, the most profound aspect of my learning came in the space of a single hour while listening to one lecturer describe his encounter with death.

On the Saturday morning of the Scleroderma Foundation's 2013 National Patient Education Conference, I'd planned to stay in my hotel room until it was time to give my noon presentation to support-group leaders at our annual luncheon. My nerves were frayed from air travel and too little sleep. Having dressed early, I tried, unsuccessfully, to relax. As I paced the hotel room, a close friend who'd traveled with me lay on her bed looking over the schedule of speakers for the day.

"We have time," she said. "Let's go hear that Botieri guy."

Hoping for an easy distraction, I let her coax me out the door.

Andrew Botieri had already begun speaking when we arrived. Slim and wiry, he appeared to be around the same age as my slim and wiry fifty-one-year-old son. His easy manner drew me in. He seemed almost carefree as he spoke about growing up in Massachusetts in a large, loving Italian family. After moving to the West Coast, he built a successful business. He spoke about how much he enjoyed his work friends, his house, and playing guitar at weekend gigs.

From the rear of the small conference room where we sat, I could see the narrowing around his mouth and the inward curling of his fingers, two common physical changes due to scleroderma. I wondered how many more years he would be able to play the guitar. Moving freely about the platform and speaking without notes, he seemed less worried about his future than I about mine. Although many of us experience similar symptoms, there's no rule for how this disease will progress. Many patients attending these conferences are indistinguishable from fully able-bodied persons. Others are reliant on oxygen and/or wheelchairs. Sadly, some of the more seriously handicapped people are the young adults.

Andrew's medical crisis began about a year after his diagnosis. One morning, on a day he was scheduled to meet with a kidney doctor, he woke up weak, confused, and temporarily blind. By the time a friend brought him to the nephrologists' office, Andrew's kidneys had already shut down, and he suffered a seizure on the spot. He was taken to the hospital with dangerously high blood pressure, which contributed to a brain hemorrhage. Respiratory failure led to the necessity of mechanical life support, and a medically induced coma was ordered to protect Andrew's brain from further damage.

Andrew's family in Massachusetts received news from his doctors that there was little hope for their son's recovery. A friend stayed with him in the hospital until, after many airport delays, his parents were able to make the cross-country flight. News about his life-threatening situation spread. Relatives and close associates formed a communication network. Visibly moved, Andrew told how business colleagues from all over the country had taken time to pray for him.

As Andrew described the terror of his organs beginning to shut down, a terrible heaviness came over me, something that was distinctly different from mere travel fatigue and a sleepless night. Its locus was in my chest. Listening to Andrew's every word, I knew that what I was experiencing was not an intellectual thing, that there was no chance of my escaping into thought. Tracking his descent into unconsciousness, I felt the shock of my own mortality.

As pastor, I'd given only cursory attention to the physical reality of death. How many times had I begun the season of Lent by imposing ashes on hands and foreheads? How many times had I stood at the head of caskets in churches and graveyards, proclaiming, "Ashes to ashes, dust to dust?" It had always felt natural to weep with members of my congregations during their grieving. As sheep-shepherd, friend-pastor, I knew we were safe with God.

Andrew's discussion of his medical crisis hit me harder than anything I'd ever felt for a stranger. Although, in thinking it over now, I can recall feeling that same heaviness when a mass murder occurred in the town where I grew up. I also felt it while mourning the loss of a man I had no business loving and at my younger cousin's funeral, even though we'd had little contact since childhood.

The pull to descend into such sorrow, even to want to die with another person from unbearable grief, is well known. There are many tales of people throwing themselves into loved ones' graves. My lack of any recognizable history with Andrew offered me no protection: I reacted as though his medical crisis were happening to my best friend or my child; it caused me to consider whether there may be more to our empathic feelings than we realize, particularly when they seem to transcend our common relationships and social boundaries.

Andrew's descent into his coma, and mine into that deeply empathic state, brought to mind the church's ancient creeds that declare Jesus' descent into hell before his ascension into heaven. I've always taken courage from that idea. To me, it says that Jesus, both human and divine, let himself go down into the hell place, taking a free fall into the dark matter of infinite universes.

I never actually *chose* to fall into Andrew's temporary Hades. My spirit, either on its own or in obedience to some mysterious directive, became willing to companion Andrew, my new stranger-friend.

Who would believe that on a July morning in Atlanta, at a convention of more than 600 patients, families, pharmaceutical reps, and medical experts, I would find myself all tangled up in a Good Friday metaphor? It occurred according to no prescribed ritual. A man afflicted with scleroderma simply painted a picture of what had happened to him. My initial response arrived wordlessly, almost entirely by way of visceral awareness, a wringing of the insides.

I can recall many Good Fridays when I sat in the back of a church and studied a finely chiseled stone frieze or carved wood figures that depicted Jesus in the walk to his death. I never managed to experience deeply what the church calls the Stations of the Cross. Although I sat silent in a pew for more than one of those three-hour-long services that mark Jesus' dying, my involvement amounted to little more than voluntary obedience. I confess my mind wandered.

Andrew's walk through the valley became, for me, an invitation to understand death and life more clearly. This would require me to not only watch Jesus carry his cross or try to carry my own but to test the weight of the wood, to smell it. I would have to see my own blood falling into the rough grain. Once, when I was a patient in the emergency room, I saw my blood, lots of it, falling from my face into a towel.

I may never again have to ask why Jesus had to die and what it meant for him or for anyone to hang from a tree. Crucifixion isn't a myth, nor is it an exclusively historical event. It's also not a horror reserved only for Christians. The crucified ones, today and forever, are every true religion's grief. To think that we who are loved and commanded to love, fail again and again to join together to care for those whom others cast aside. Instead of revering and preserving life, we compete, steal, and kill. We enrage our planet—not only with abuse of its resources but with our careless ideologies. We don't dare to admit how much we share others' religious values, rituals, practices, and, sometimes, the most deadly misunderstandings.

Jesus helps me in looking outward from my core to accept with certainty that all persons on this round earth are the keepers of our sisters and brothers—even those whom we will never meet.

Andrew Botieri wrote a book about scleroderma.[13] After describing his collapse, he included pages his sister Karen wrote about her friend Pat's mysterious experience. Pat felt an urgency to do something to help Andrew. The night after Andrew's hospital admission, Pat happened to notice a phone number for prayer requests in her copy of her daily worship guide. Pat lit a candle, called the number, and asked for a prayer for Andrew's recovery. After hearing the first few words of the spoken prayer, Pat's ears stopped working. She reported feeling

---

[13] Botieri, Andrew Louis. *A Celebration of Life: A Story of Hope, a Miracle, and the Power of Attitude.* Plymouth: Nino-Ida Publishing. 2014. 21–22. Print.

strange, as though she were being "transported to [Andrew's] room thousands of miles away."[14] She saw Andrew lying in a hospital bed near a window. A robed man stood over him, passing his hand above his body as though he was performing a magic trick. When the man turned around to look at Pat, his face was Christ-like. As the vision faded, Pat tuned into the voice on the phone just in time to hear the words "He will be healed."[15] The next day, Andrew woke from his two-day coma.

I admire Andrew's faith. His guardian angels are specific. One is his cousin and namesake, Andrew, who died at eighteen. Andrew said that his cousin appeared to him when he was coming out of his coma, in great pain, and essentially alone. Another angel who's always been on his side in this life and beyond is his grandfather. Andrew remained confident that both of his guardian angels were watching over him during his illness, praying for him as any one of us would pray, but without earthly distractions.

During his recovery, Andrew decided to move back to the town in Massachusetts where he grew up. There, refreshed by memories of his childhood and supported by his family and childhood friends, his healing continued. Gradually, he became strong enough to return to his work and to play his guitar at weekend gigs.

Andrew's engagement with us, his audience, that morning during the conference reinforced my appreciation of presence— the presence of the preacher, the presence of God, the presence

---

[14]  ibid., 22
[15]  ibid., 22

of reckless hope. Andrew persevered. He never gave up on himself or on his purpose. He had hope when there was no sign of it. Watching and listening to him, I continued to marvel at how spiritual strength is revealed in the quality of a person's presence. It wasn't so much the words he said as it was the passion that produced them.

Nearly twenty-eight years ago a handful of parishioners and I climbed to a church on a mountaintop in New Jersey to get a glimpse of Mother Teresa of Calcutta. I found a spot on the path directly in back of someone in a wheelchair. As Mother Teresa walked past the crowd on her way to the church, my view was unimpeded.

The mountaintop sanctuary had seats for invited guests only, so a hundred or more of us sat outside on the grass. The saint's words were amplified over the sound system, but nothing she said touched my heart. *Seeing* her was everything. This small, thin woman, dark from the sun and wrinkled from age, was simply herself. We were the same, simply ourselves, every one of us as we remained sitting on the grass together, so silently, so respectfully, in the light of our amazement.

We are not what we have accomplished, no matter how impressive. We are not the disease with which we have been diagnosed. We are not the body beautiful or the body ravaged that we put on display or attempt to hide from the world. We are humans related to one another by virtue of our humanity and that spark of divinity in each person, a Judeo-Christian concept, but one that goes far beyond the label.

During a year that included many setbacks, Andrew kept a loving eye on those around him and on his goal of returning to what he loves to do. He's working again but not slavishly. He plays his guitar on weekends when he's well enough. Andrew is someone who claims to be a workaholic. He knows that when work is both play and helpful to others, there's no downside. There is, however, the need to pace himself and care for his body, which has hidden weaknesses. (Does a body exist that doesn't have hidden weaknesses?) And there is forever the need to take time every day to renew his inner life.

When Andrew refers to the importance of attitude, he's talking about much more than grasping the most positive outcome and holding on to it. He's talking about looking outside ourselves and toward the good we intend to do with our temporarily healed bodies. Surely, caring for those who are carrying the heaviest burdens is a first step.

While he was a patient on dialysis, Andrew befriended his fellow patients in his unit. After he was taken off his blood-purifying regimen, he went back to the hospital regularly to greet and converse with those undergoing the same treatment. Dialysis units are, for most people, the last stop. Patients try to read or sleep, but so often they seem isolated and despairing. Andrew found ways to make them smile.

Andrew and I shared a handshake and a few words at the close of his talk, an event that left me shaken but that I had no time to process. I went immediately to the room where I was scheduled to speak, still quite early and, as usual, over-prepared. Although my presentation wasn't as powerful as Andrew's, it went remarkably well. After the community lunch and conversation, I slept most of the afternoon.

On Sunday morning, I sat among several hundred attendees at one of the long, narrow tables dotted with the hotel's coffee cups and plastic water glasses, listening vaguely to a presentation I'd heard before in another setting. My traveling companion was still upstairs packing. My bags were stored at the desk of the concierge.

I looked up from my papers to see Andrew standing in front of me on the other side of the narrow table. He must have received the message I sent through the conference grapevine asking for his contact information. He was bending toward me slightly, handing me his business card. As his eyes caught mine, I saw distinctly, in his features, a living icon of the Christ.

I'd always wondered what it means to see Christ in another person. In seminary we were asked to try to do this. I thought, perhaps rightly, that this might be an exercise for holding, in conscience, the value of every human being. I practiced this and still do, although I never again saw the face of Christ as clearly as I did in Andrew's face that day.

## Postscript

When a miracle is seen or experienced, it is useful only if it takes us to a place of greater trust in the possibilities for our lives and the lives of our neighbors on this small and increasingly fragile planet.

# The Healing of Sandy Coe

S andy sat in what we came to call the prayer chair, a plain wooden chair that one of us pulled into the center of a circle we made near the front of the sanctuary. Standing around her, we took turns reading aloud from the healing liturgy since Pastor Craig, despite his thick lenses, was unable to read the small print.

The Wednesday morning service was Pastor Craig's idea. It began as a small gathering to pray for Sandy and her family. Knowing my interest in healing prayer, the young pastor invited me to join him and his Lutheran parishioners for the service. Barring medical appointments or heavy snowstorms, Sandy, her husband, and their younger adult daughter came to the service regularly. Pastor Craig would read from scripture and give a homily about how God wills our wholeness. His speaking from memory, rather than from notes, made him wonderfully present.

When he asked for Sandy's prayer request, she said, "I

want prayers for the healing of my cancer." Her voice had the confidence of someone who knows how to gain divine attention.

She said those words—"I want prayers for the healing of my cancer"—when her illness was first diagnosed. She said them during remission and she said them when the bad cells seemed to be gone for good. I heard beauty in her repeated phrase but missed the logic of it. Logic would dictate that she change her request to reflect the changes in her condition. Yet, whether enduring trials or enjoying periods of relief, Sandy kept her prayer the same.

One day, Pastor Craig tried encouraging her to amend her request.

"And your arthritis, Sandy," he said. "Let's not forget to pray for your arthritis!"

But Sandy didn't seem to care about her arthritis. Her concern, spoken or not, was focused on the illness that eventually returned to take her from us.

When the healing service began to include Communion as well, Pastor Craig received permission from his bishop to allow me to be the celebrant—the person to offer the Bread and the Cup—during the weeks he traveled. Offering the bread and the cup had become a rare occurrence for me after I began my work as a full-time counselor. I'll never forget those mornings as celebrant—how, after our prayers had enfolded Sandy, I leaned over to draw the sign of the cross on her forehead. Holding the round tin of fragrant oil in my palm, inhaling the scent of myrrh spiraling upward in a thin vapor, I could feel it in my bones: this place, this small circle of peace, was where I, where each one of us in this group, was meant to be.

Our ongoing prayers for Sandy's deliverance continued. Aware that she had a killer disease, she also knew that she had witnesses who loved her. We watched when she began to have trouble standing. We watched when her coordination and speech began to fail. Her husband placed his hands next to ours on her back and shoulders while Pastor Craig's hands, or mine, rested on her head. On the days when no pastor could be present, one of the church's two deacons filled in. At the close of the service, there was always someone to bless each one of us with oil.

When Pastor Craig was called to another ministry, we missed him. I missed our collaboration, our discussions, and his sense of humor. I still remember the way he walked around the neighborhood in a dark suit and his clerical collar, his white cane scanning the sidewalk. This legally blind pastor had added an important visual clue to his identity: he wore a large black cowboy hat, which evoked his sense of play. (Yes, play! Real fun is no stranger to some of the most dedicated saints.)

Our little group continued to expand and contract over time. While Sandy still came to sit in the prayer chair, others sat there as well, including most of the pastors who followed Craig. As for Sandy, she stayed on with us until the very end of her journey.

Everyone who knew her would agree that Sandy enjoyed life—every minute of it—especially, perhaps, when it seemed to be slipping away. She wasted no time on regrets. Her good days allowed her to enjoy theater and musical events, and, as long as she was able, to help out at church and with visiting hospital patients. Her resilience, sustained by faith, helped carry her, and us, through the five years of her illness. At home, she taught her husband to cook and even joked about fixing him up with someone nice for when she was gone.

The little church's successive pastors began to move away from the formal liturgy during the Wednesday morning service. Those of us serving as celebrants had memorized the core of the Communion liturgy and knew to ask for healing without limiting it to the physical kind. We learned to trust the prayers we prayed in our hearts—to surround and fill Sandy with God's Love, ensuring her journey would be a safe one.

Occasional one-time visitors showed up at our service, as did people who stayed for months or even years. One Wednesday morning, a Baptist pastor came by to ask how many healings had come about as a result of our prayers. With eyes downcast, I considered our lack of statistics, but Sandy spoke up.

"Well, there's me," she said. "There's my healing!"

We stood mute as she told about her nearly two-year remission. While she was speaking, she knew—we all knew—that the red-and-yellow snake-like clusters were winding in and around her brain. Yet she described her remission as though it were a permanent gift. Sandy had received the healing of extra time and the grace to enjoy it.

The week before she died, Sandy called to tell me her oncologist recommended that she begin hospice care, where a trained volunteer would come to her home to visit and pray with her if she wished.

"I'm not ready for that," she said with crisp impatience.

I'm sure Sandy was aware that, for many, the hospice experience offers one of the gentlest possible ways of leaving the earth. A musician, who plays her harp at a local hospice, brings beauty to the dying person's last days or hours. As for Sandy's stark reaction, I believe she wanted me to agree with her that she was just fine, which I did, and which she was, in more ways than one. She was still celebrating life.

A week later, over Memorial Day weekend, Sandy's older daughter drove up from Baltimore, and the two of them had a good visit. The very next day, Sandy expressed uncertainty about being able to navigate much longer without a walker. Her husband went immediately to borrow one from the town's fire department. Upon his return, he found Sandy sleeping so soundly in the recliner that he couldn't wake her. Lying down on the nearby couch, he listened to the cadence of her breathing as it became slower and more labored. Against the silence of a late summer afternoon, he heard her take her last breath.

I imagined Sandy's body relaxed in the big chair, her spirit stepping out of it quite easily, as though she had been about to take a walk down a street lined with green trees, a street flooded with sunlight. There, Sandy, healed of every illness, walked through that green valley into the company of the saints of light, the saints we sing about but very seldom see.

At the time of this writing, the weekday services continue.

Sandy's husband found a loving companion, but on Wednesday mornings he comes alone to be with us.

Recently, a deacon took over as celebrant. So much and so little has changed over the years. We read the psalm responsively and meditate on it together. We hold hands while standing in a circle during the Lord's Prayer, and then we make our individual thanksgivings and supplications. In the pauses we say, "Lord, in your mercy, hear our prayer." Passing the peace is the same tender jumble of hugs and bumping of arms it has always been, but now we laugh at our less-coordinated gestures. From time to time we remember and speak of Sandy, whose needs first inspired Pastor Craig to call us together.

The Communion elements have changed a little. A gluten-free cube is consecrated alongside the wheaten hosts. A sip of the Lutheran wine still burns my Methodist throat all the way down to my toes. And, lastly, one or two of us takes a turn sitting in the prayer chair to ask for healing—for ourselves, for a friend, for the world. A modest ceremony, this.

The body weakens. The world is in travail. Yet God is with us. Our hands, even with their arthritic changes, make beautiful designs resting of the back of our neighbor in the prayer chair. We inhale the scent of myrrh as we feel the touch of the invisible cross being drawn with oil on our foreheads. In a few minutes, we will leave for breakfast in bodies that continue, amazingly, to carry us where we want to go.

Printed in the United States
By Bookmasters